JUST JERKY

THE COMPLETE GUIDE TO MAKING IT

Mary Bell

♻ Printed on recycled paper with soy-based ink in the United States of America

The Dry Store Publishing Company
3810 Odana Road, Madison, Wisconsin 53711
www.drystore.com
marytbell@drystore.com
FAX 507-467-2694

Just Jerky / Mary Bell
Includes Index
ISBN 0-9653572-0-1
Library of Congress TX 4-358-254

First Edition
       7 8 9 10

Cover Design: Ira Newman
Illustrator: Dale Mann
Editor: Annie Beckmann
Book Design: Mary Jo Exley

Note: Check with dehydrator, smoker and oven manufacturers for operating and maintenance directions.

A good book for jerky fans everywhere

". . . Mary Bell is the undisputed queen of the dehydrator, the holder of a reliable jerky recipe for every occasion and, with her new book, **Just Jerky**, an answer to every jerk's question."

George Hesselberg, Wisconsin State Journal

Discovering this book was like finding a gold mine

"No more searching through the back pages of assorted camp cookbooks for jerky recipes."

Boris Swidersky, Bushwhacker Magazine (Canada)

'Just Jerky' is a real gem

"Mary Bell guides the reader through every imaginable type of jerky from the more common varieties made from game or domestic animals to more unusual vegetarian, fish or ground meat versions."

Ginger Johnston, Portland Oregonian

Jerky book tasty delight

"**Just Jerky** . . .is not only an eye-opener to anyone who has ever made venison jerky, but your stomach will growl in anticipation, too."

Bill Baab, The Augusta (GA) Chronicle

'Just Jerky' offers deer hunters plenty of recipes to chew on

"Here's a do-it-yourself guide to making your own jerky, just in time to make good use of the venison bagged in the recent deer hunting season."

Karen Herzog, Milwaukee (WI) Journal Sentinel

CONTENTS

Foreword by John Kvasnicka

FOREWORD

I've made jerky from wild turkey, bear, pheasant, antelope, deer, goose, moose and elk. Deer meat is still my favorite, although moose and elk make good jerky, too.

Last year, my wife Colleen and I took two venison hindquarters—sliced the meat thin, cut it into strips and marinated it in everything from Mary Bell's teriyaki to her onion concoction. Every recipe Mary Bell has shared with us has been great.

Four weekends a year, 11 members of our family get together for campouts. We cook over an open pit and snack on dried fruits and jerky. We think of these outings as experiential learning where we reach consensus and peace of mind as a family. And we're always more likely to reflect around a campfire with a piece of jerky in hand. I have yet to be in a camp that doesn't like jerky. It's a staff of life, like bread and water. When you make it yourself, it's one of those foods that brings you closer to nature and connects you to your ancestors who survived by living off the land.

John Kvasnicka
Executive Director, Minnesota Deer Hunters Association, 1989 - 1996

INTRODUCTION

True confessions. I was once a vegetarian. It was the early '70s when I decided vegetarianism was a gentler, cheaper way for a single mother of two to live.

The three of us had been vegetarians about a year when my 5-year-old son shouted out from the back seat of the car one day, "I don't care if you're a vegetarian, Mom, I want a hamburger." I heard him loud and clear and drove to the nearest burger joint.

It was at a time when I was struggling to take responsibility for securing our food supply. We had a large garden and I dried food as a method of preservation. Once my son let me know he wanted meat in our diet, I knew I had to develop the skills to bag my own. That's when I joined an archery league. One night, friends from my archery league brought over a deer and we butchered it at my kitchen table. I learned to cook venison and began making jerky.

When I started drying food, I began outdoors with a stack of old window screens with abysmal success. Oven-drying was a bit more reliable. It was the electric dehydrator, however, that opened the door to successful food drying.

As my passion for food drying grew, I sold food dehydrators at home and garden shows, fairs and sport shows. I promoted the concept of food drying in North and Central America. I wrote two books on the subject, *Dehydration Made Simple* (Magic Mill, 1981) and *Mary Bell's Complete Dehydrator Cookbook* (William Morrow, 1994). I continue to teach classes and talk about food drying to just about anybody who'll listen. The more I learn, the more it fuels my curiosity.

In my travels, people often hit me with a barrage of questions about making jerky. Is jerky hard to make? How do you know when jerky is dry? What's a good marinade? Is it safe to eat? Making jerky, I soon learned, is why many people purchase food dehydrators.

If you buy a lot of jerky, if you hunt, fish, hike, or if you're just looking for a healthy low-fat snack or perhaps you're one of those people who just took a new dehydrator out of the box and it is sitting on the kitchen counter and your family is yelling "Dad, jerky, please," this book is for you.

I've provided information on how to make jerky out of strips of meat or fish, how to make ground meat jerky, as well as making jerky from non-meat products. I've addressed safety concerns. For a broader understanding, I included a history. Then, hold onto your taste buds, the best jerky marinades I've ever tasted are included. Plus there are delicious and fun recipes to use jerky in cooking and baking—there's jerky stew, jerky bread, jerky cake, jerky frosting and even jerky ice cream. I've spent years collecting recipes, suggestions, tips, techniques and ideas from a variety of sources. I've experimented and tested every recipe in this book. I've dried jerky in dehydrators, in smokers and in the oven.

This book is more than just instructions and recipes—it represents a community of people. Throughout these pages you will find friends who shared their wisdom and experiences with me. Many of the jerkies and recipes for using them were taste-tested by family, staff at L'Etoile, friends and show audiences. My husband Joe was the lucky one who tested the vegetarian jerkies. He's a great guy with a good heart. Odessa Piper, owner of L'Etoile, a restaurant in Madison, Wisconsin, opened her kitchen for testing and created the opportunity for Chef Gene Gowan to help with the marinades and superb flavor blendings. Editor Annie Beckmann was a treat to work with throughout all stages of this book's evolution. Doris Mueller scoured the library system and found helpful information. Gratitude is expressed to the Don Engebretson family for their help and guidance.

My determination to be self-sufficient has turned into a life philosophy. Food represents our most intimate link and essential connection to the land. It is our source of health and vitality, the centerpiece of family, ethnic and community traditions. Food reflects who we are and what we value. I believe the more we assume responsibility for our food supply and reduce our dependence on the food industry, the more we lessen our impact on the planet. Taking food from the land around us and preserving it in our homes provides us with a thoughtful alternative. Drying meat and fish is intrinsic to this approach.

It's been more than 25 years since my son Eric shouted for a burger from the back seat. Last fall he started working at an archery shop and within six months he was hitting the bull's-eye square on at 20 yards 95 percent of the time. And every once in awhile, my son and other friends still bring me hunks of raw meat to try out new jerky marinades.

Mary Bell

ONE

WHAT IT IS

THE MEANING OF JERKY

Jerky has many meanings. As a verb, it relates to movement. To twitch is to jerk. A quick pull, twist, push, thrust or throw is a jerk. An unexpected muscular contraction caused by a reflex action is a jerk. Convulsive or spasmodic movements are jerky, as are sudden starts and stops.

Speech isn't without its jerks. To utter anything with sharp gasps is to jerk out.

Jerkin sounds like slang, but in the 16th century, it was an article of clothing—a short, close-fitting, often sleeveless coat or jacket. In more recent times, a jerkin became a short, sleeveless vest worn by women. A jerkin is also a type of hawk, the male of the gerfalcon.

The noun jerker has two meanings. One is a British customs agent who searches vessels for unentered goods. One who, or that which jerks is also known as a jerker.

That brings us to jerks. Steve Martin starred in the movie "*The Jerk.*" The Larks sang and millions danced to "The Jerk." A real jerk, the kind we've all encountered, is a person regarded as stupid, dull, maybe eccentric. Jerks—and jerkers, for that matter—can come from jerkwater towns.

However, jerky is most usefully meat preserved by slicing it into strips and drying it in the sun, over a fire or in a dehydrator, smoker or oven. This North American food was referred to as *charqui*, pronounced "sharkey" in Spanish. Eventually this dried meat became known as jerky or jerked beef. Dry meats are sometimes called jerk. Caribbean cooks popularized a style of cooking that typically calls for a marinade laced with allspice. That's jerk, too. With all this in mind, I dedicate this book to the jerk in us all.

Jerkin

WHAT'S JERKY?

Jerky is raw meat that's flavored and dried.

I've talked to people who make jerky from kangaroo, rattlesnake, coyote, ostrich, mountain sheep, whale, wild duck and wild goose, blue gills, smelt and carp. I've read about liver, heart and even blood jerky. Originally venison meant any game but today it is synonymous with deer meat. Venison actually includes elk, moose, antelope and reindeer.

The following is by no means a comprehensive listing, but it should give you an idea of some of the foods you can jerk.

Domestic and wild meats include: beef, buffalo, venison, elk, moose, antelope, rabbit, lamb, goat. **Poultry** includes: chicken, turkey, duck, goose, ostrich, emu. **Low-fat salt water fish** include: sole, flounder, halibut, pollock, tuna, rock cod. **Fresh water fish** include: sunfish, crappies, perch, walleye, bass, smelt. **Fish with higher oil content** include: salmon, trout, catfish.

Commercial products include: luncheon meats, pepperoni, venison sausage, ham, salami, pastrami, smoked turkey and chicken breasts.

Jerky can be made from fresh, frozen or canned meat or fish that is cut into strips or ground. It's also possible to make jerky with soy bean products. Once seasoned, jerky is dried in a dehydrator or an oven and/or smoked. Most meat and fish contain 60 to 70 per cent water (fruits and vegetables contain 80 to 90 percent). When foods are dried, their water content is reduced to between 3 and 10 percent. In general, dried foods are reduced to between one half and one fourth of their original quantity, both in weight and volume.

WHY WOULD YOU WANT TO MAKE YOUR OWN?

When you make jerky, you select the quality of meat and flavorings used. Then think about the price. A single ounce of commercial jerky runs $1 to $2. At $32 a pound, it costs more than spiny lobster from the coldest waters of Maine. Homemade jerky is not only delicious, but is a better product for less money. A pound of fresh meat ($2 to $3), a cup of teriyaki sauce (50 cents), and a few pennies for electricity translates into 6 to 8 ounces of homemade jerky. Making homemade jerky gives you more control over the use of chemicals, preservatives and salt.

A quick check of a storebought jerky label will show the differences. Commercial ingredients often include: water, salt, corn syrup, dextrose, spices, smoke flavoring, monosodium glutamate, sodium erythrobate, garlic powder, sodium nitrate, BHA, BHT, potassium sorbate and citric acid. Commercial jerkies are made from strips or formed ground meats—usually about ⅛-inch thick. Textures vary from hard and tough to moist and tender.

For many people, the first introduction to jerky is what they buy. The popularity of jerky continues to soar. Over the past year, total supermarket jerky sales in the United States reached $37.2 million, $34.7 million of which was in beef jerky alone, according to Nielsen Market Research data. "Jerky is a growing market," says Deb Willford, market research analyst for the Oberto Sausage Company in Kent, Washington. Oberto's retail jerky sales are roughly $20 million annually, Willford estimates. According to SNACKWorld magazine, the market demand for meat snacks has been explosive, making it the fastest growing segment in the snack food industry.

HISTORY OF DRYING

Humans have benefited from dried foods since the Cro-Magnon era. Sun and wind fostered the first dried foods. Early people copied the drying process they observed in nature. Dried grasses, dried seeds, dried fruits and nuts were gathered and stored. Animals cached their game in trees where it dried in the wind. Our ancestors responded to the same hunger we feel. They needed to eat and feed their families just like we do.

Dried meat and salted fish, along with bread and beans, have been staples for centuries. Long before the luxury of electricity, fish and poultry were salted and sun-dried on the banks of the Nile. Stored grains, berries and meats enriched the soups during hard winters. Few fresh vegetables could be harvested from frozen ground, with the exception of the inner bark of trees and occasional greens such as watercress.

Whale meat, octopus, snails, mice, locusts and other insects were among the first dried foods. Egyptians salted and dried game. Spaniards filleted mules, cut them into paper-thin strips and sun-dried them. Chinese salted and sun-dried snakes. People

dried food to use when fresh food was not available. Sun, wind and smoke from a fire provided ways to remove water from foods and preserve them.

Dried fish continues to be a principal food source. With more than 20,000 species of fish—most of them edible—it's clear why fish have been called "the wheat of the sea."

Native Americans recognized the value of setting up camp near the seacoasts, lakes, rivers and streams. Shellfish, crustaceans and sluggish fish were scooped up by hand. Fishing and hunting became easier once spears and harpoons were available.

Archaeological digs offer clues that Native Americans dried bison, elk, deer, antelope, wolf, coyote, badger, beaver, fox, rabbits, squirrels, salmon, catfish, cod, perch, carp, prairie chicken, grouse, eagles, geese, turtles and snakes. Our ancestors had a wholesome, diverse diet.

As the white community spread westward, Native Americans sold them pemmican, a high protein food made with ground dried meat, berries and fat. (See pemmican recipes on pages 104-107.)

HOW THE NATIVE AMERICANS MADE THEIR OWN JERKY

Right after a hunt, hunters brought fresh meat to camp where it was cut and dried. The women packed the dried meat in skin bags (parfleches). Because bull flesh was tough, and calf flesh crumbled when dried (making it harder to store), buffalo cows were used to make jerky. Bones were boiled for marrow fat, which was kept in bladders and used to make pemmican. In some tribes, the fresh skins were crafted into round, bathtub-like vessels called bull boats.

Once the meat or fish was cut into strips, there were several ways it was dried into jerky. Smoke added flavor and helped keep hungry creatures away. Hanging strips over the campfire took advantage of the dry circulating air. Sometimes a tepee became a smokehouse. Strips of fish were placed beside the fire to dry.

Sometimes partially dried fish fillets were placed on a sheet of clean birch bark and mashed smooth. Maple sugar was added to both sweeten and preserve the mixture which was stored in birch bark containers.

Smoked, dried salmon, is still prepared the way it was centuries ago. Fresh fish strips are dry cured or soaked in brine, then smoked until dry over a fire of alderwood or dried in the sun until they become chewy.

For centuries, cleaned fish and meat have been packed in crocks of salted water. The brine draws moisture out of the soaking food and salt replaces the water inside the food. Within a couple of days, the foods are immersed in water. Once brining is complete, the liquid is drained off and the fish or meat is dried.

5

THE DRYING STAGE

One of my favorite books, *Buffalo Bird Woman's Garden*, details how a woman of the Hidatsa tribe that lived along the Missouri River, planted, harvested and preserved food. Drying meat, fruit and vegetables was very important. Each lodge in a village had its own drying stage. It was a place of respect and honor because of the food that was dried there and the way of life it provided.

Strangers and children were not allowed on the drying stage. The drying stage floor was about 30 feet long and 12 feet wide. Women built the platforms from cottonwood timbers that were cut in the summer, peeled of their bark and left through the winter to dry. When the stage was constructed, the men raised the heavy posts and the forks to support the floor beams.

Strips of raw meat were hung on drying rods. A drying rod was a pole about two inches thick by 13 feet long, with ends that projected over the rail at each end. On sunny, windy days, fresh meat would dry in 48 to 72 hours. To speed up drying, sometimes a low fire would be lit under the stage floor.

Drying Stage

6

TWO

SAFETY

IS IT OK TO EAT?

Jerky is generally raw meat that's been flavored and dried. This often raises fears that may, in fact, be unfounded. If the plan is to stuff unrefrigerated meat in a backpack, jerky is safer to eat than cured ham, smoked turkey breast or a roast beef sandwich.

Once the internal temperature of meat reaches 145 degrees F. and stays at that temperature for at least ten minutes, salmonella, E. coli and trichinosis are no longer threatening, according to Dr. Art Maurer, professor of poultry products technology at the University of Wisconsin-Madison. Maurer says jerky has an overlap of three safety factors going for it. First, most dehydrators—and most means those capable of sustaining a temperature of 145 degrees—are hot enough to kill most bacteria. Second, salt levels in jerky are higher than in other uncooked meats. Third, the drying process eliminates more than 90 percent of the water, the medium that bacteria needs to grow.

Although rare, trichinosis has been found in pork products and game meats such as bear and walrus. To eliminate the parasite trichinosis, a constant temperature of 135 degrees for five to 10 minutes is sufficient. Freezing also destroys the parasite if the raw meat is held at -20 degrees F. for six days.

Making jerky engages the senses. You smell the marinade, feel the meat's texture for dryness and, to ensure shelf-life safety, you rely on sight. If jerky is not dried enough, it can develop mold. When mold is found on jerky, all foods stored together in the

same container must be discarded. Don't confuse a white ash on the surface of dried meats with mold, though. During the dehydration process, liquid components come to the surface and dry. That white ash film is apt to be crystallized salt, which is not a hazard.

A teaspoon of salt added to a pound of meat is no more than flavoring. However, when the meat is dried, that teaspoon of salt inhibits bacteria. Salty ingredients—soy, Worcestershire, pickling and curing salt—become preservatives.

It's best to use pickling and curing salt rather than table salt. Avoid rock salt, which contains too many impurities. Table salt has iodine, which may cause an avoidable chemical reaction if the meat marinates in an aluminum container.

STORAGE

According to Maurer, the shelf life is dependent on moisture content, packaging and storage temperature. The water activity in dried jerky will be very low, so most bacteria, yeast and many molds will not grow. The better the package, the longer the shelf life. The colder the temperature, the longer the shelf life. So it appears that a properly dried jerky product with good packaging should have a room temperature shelf life of at least half a year, Maurer says.

Like any other dried food, jerky lasts longest when stored in airtight containers in a cool, dry place. Airtight containers include jars with tight-fitting lids or sealable plastic bags. Even though our ancestors dried meat and fish and kept it from year to year without refrigeration, I recommend storing jerky in the refrigerator or freezer, especially if you want to keep it longer than one month. Storage life can be affected by humidity and temperature of the storage area. I have kept jerky in a jar on the counter for several months. It doesn't taste as fresh as when I keep it in the refrigerator or freezer. This is especially true for thicker pieces of jerky. When jerky contains fat, it has more potential to turn rancid and shouldn't be stored at room temperature.

Moisture content is jerky's biggest contamination factor. There's greater surface contamination with poor packaging. Botulism is very rare, although it's found in fish once in awhile, says Maurer. However, botulism only grows in the absence of air. Jerky's not prone to botulism unless it's vacuum packed improperly, then not refrigerated. Many commercial jerkies are vacuum packed.

When making jerky, it's always a good idea to label jerky packages with name and date of drying process. I write the type of jerky on masking tape, put it on the marinating container, then transfer it to the drying trays. When the jerky is dry, I put this same label on the storage container.

When packaging jerky that feels oily, wrap it in paper towels and let cool for a couple of hours. The toweling will absorb excess oil. Discard the oily paper toweling and wrap again in clean paper towels. Place the wrapped jerky in a container. This will help prevent rancidity and encourage longer storage. If it smells rancid or if mold forms in the container, discard it.

TEMPERATURE

All raw meats must be dried at temperatures of 145 degrees and above. The internal temperature of the meat pieces must remain at this temperature for at least 10 minutes. Check to make sure your dehydrator runs continuously at the same temperature. If you have a dehydrator that does not have a temperature control, you can still use it to dry jerky. However, once the jerky is dry, it's a good idea to put it in the oven at the lowest temperature setting for 30 minutes. When drying precooked foods, temperature isn't as important.

Although storage is a serious consideration, jerky lasts only if I have found a good hiding place or when I make serious threats to anyone with jerky breath.
A lady at one of my classes suggested her storage trick, "Wrap it in freezer paper and label it liver."

TIME

Jerky generally dries in four to 20 hours. Time varies depending on the type and wattage of the dehydrator or oven. Many factors must be taken into consideration: the amount of jerky you're making, the number of trays in a dehydrator, water content of wet jerky, size of pieces (generally ¼-inch thick and 4 to 5 inches long), humidity in the air and the temperature used. Faster drying can be accomplished by increasing the temperature. If jerky becomes too crisp, it was dried too long or the temperature was too high.

COOKING

If your dehydrator doesn't have a temperature control and there's no way to determine the drying temperature, as a safety precaution you may want to precook foods to be made into jerky.

Cooking includes steaming, braising, baking or simmering. Strips of meat or fish, including ground meat strips can be placed on cookie sheets, put in the oven for 20 minutes at 150 degrees F., then dried in a dehydrator or smoker.

Benefits of cooking prior to drying include:

- Cooking releases moisture, which shortens the drying process.

- Cooking helps eliminate fat.

- Cooking lengthens the storage life. Cooked jerky is a more stable product.

- Cooked jerky reconstitutes faster and has a better texture.

- Jerky can be made from leftover cooked meat and fish. Cut cooked Thanksgiving turkey or Easter ham into cubes or strips and place in a drying environment.

IS IT DRY YET?

Jerky darkens and shrinks when it's dry. One pound of raw meat or fish generally dries to between ⅓ and ½ pound of jerky. When testing for dryness, always feel cooled pieces—warm pieces feel more pliable. It's safer to overdry than to underdry.

"Dry" has many different meanings to people. Here's a look at how a variety of sources describe their methods for knowing when jerky is dry.

■ Squeeze a piece of dried jerky between your thumb and forefinger—you should not feel any moisture or soft spots.

■ Dry until firm, but not as crisp as a tortilla chip, not so dry that it shatters.

■ When folded in half, jerky breaks.

■ Jerky bends like a green willow.

■ It won't snap clean like a dry stick.

■ Jerky is hard to cut with a regular knife. A serrated knife or kitchen scissors work better.

FATTY ITEMS

Fat or oil does not dry. During the drying process, it beads up on the surface of the jerky. That's why it's important to cut off as much fat as possible when preparing meat and fish to make jerky. When making jerky from pork, it must be cooked and the fat removed before being dried. When you remove fat, you help eliminate more of the gamey taste.

Dog, chum and pink salmon are the least oily salmon and are best for drying in a dehydrator or oven. Any oil that beads up during drying in a dehydrator or oven must be patted off. On the other hand, when making smoked fish jerky, choose a fatty fish because oil has a tenderizing effect during smoking. In a smoker, the oil drips off and burns away.

DRYING FAT

Although I just said that fat does not dry, I came across the following interesting story. It strikes me as a type of cheese.

A 17th-century writer reported on an ancient practice of preserving fat. In the Faeroe Islands, a group of 18 islands in the North Atlantic near Iceland, mutton fat was preserved by cutting the tallow of sheep in pieces. The tallow then was allowed to rot, rendered and cut into cubes. These tallow chunks were stored in an earthen pit. The longer it was kept, the better it got—when very old, it tasted like cheese.

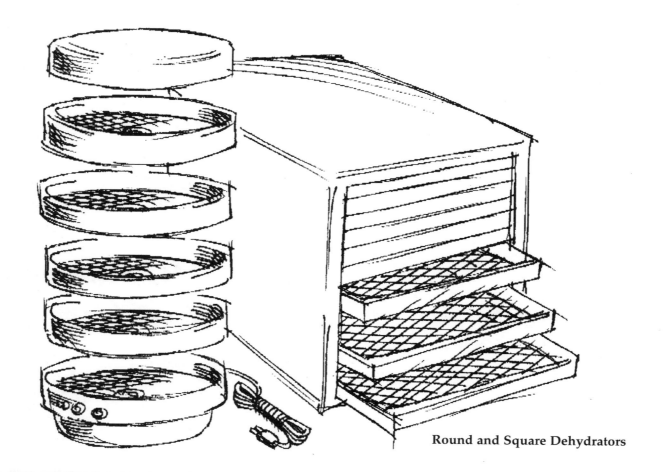

Round and Square Dehydrators

THREE

EQUIPMENT

To make jerky, water in meat or fish must be eliminated. There are several ways to do this. Jerky can be dried in electric dehydrators, in smokers, in ovens, and, for the really adventurous, with air drying. The choice may depend on space both in and outdoors, quality concerns and equipment costs.

ELECTRIC DEHYDRATORS

My first choice of equipment for making jerky is an electric dehydrator. Put food in, turn the unit on, set the temperature, and in a few hours you'll have jerky. Depending on the style of the dehydrator, the jerky may need to be turned once or twice during the drying process. You can make jerky in an electric dehydrator any time.

Reliable equipment makes the process easier and more fun. Choose an electric dehydrator that heats to at least 145 degrees F. If using a dehydrator that has a preset temperature that can't be adjusted, use a meat thermometer to make sure the temperature is high enough to make jerky.

Electric food dehydrators vary in size, style and design. They all create dry air that removes water from food. Dehydrators range in price from $30 to $300. The most popular dehydrator shape is round. The heat source and fan are on the bottom and trays are stacked on top with a lid covering the top tray. Dry air either flows up through the trays, or the dry, heated air is forced up through an opening around the outside of the trays and across each tray in a horizontal pattern. Other dehydrators are square or rectangular and

resemble microwave ovens with a front door and removable trays. This style generally has the heat source and fan at the back or on one side.

When making jerky, a good balance of both air flow and heat is critical. If the air flow is unevenly distributed in the drying chamber, trays may need to be rotated every two to four hours.

Be advised that some dehydrators have an uncovered heat coil in the bottom of the dehydrator base. When fat in drying fish and meat gets hot, it may drip onto the coil. Care must be taken with this type of dehydrator because of the fire hazard.

DEHYDRATOR ACCESSORIES

Dehydrators have accessories that make the drying process easy and more versatile. Often accessory items from one style dehydrator can be used or adapted and used with other dehydrators. A special accessory sheet called a **mesh** (above right) or **insert sheet** helps minimize dripping from one tray to the one below it. I will refer to this as a mesh sheet. Dehydrator trays have holes that allow air to flow in and around drying foods. If these holes are large enough, small pieces (such as pieces of ground meat jerky) and marinating liquids may fall or drip through. The mesh sheet has much smaller holes which helps prevent this. This sheet also keeps foods from sticking to the trays, making clean-up easier.

Another helpful dehydrator accessory is called a **roll-up, leather** or **fruit roll-up sheet**. I will refer to this as a roll-up sheet. It is a solid plastic tray liner that fits on top of the drying tray. It is generally used for holding pureed foods to make fruit or vegetable leathers. Put the roll-up sheet under the mesh sheet when drying items that are particularly drippy or have a lot of fat or oil. The roll-up sheet is also helpful when making jerky from ground meats. (See pages 73-77 for more information on ground meat jerky.)

EXTRUDING DEVICES

There are several new products that extrude ground meat and other ground foods. Please refer to pages 75-77 for more information on these products and for directions on how to use them.

STILL MORE HELPFUL STUFF

Here are some household items that come in handy for jerky making.

If your oven, smoker or dehydrator does not have an accurate temperature control, you may want to purchase a meat thermometer with a stainless steel point to check the internal temperatures of the drying jerky. These are generally available at hardware stores or kitchen shops.

A mortar and pestle is especially efficient for grinding dried herbs and spices. A blender or food processor is useful for pureeing. Use heavy-duty masking tape and a waterproof pen for labeling.

MAKING JERKY IN A DEHYDRATOR

For safety's sake, when putting food into a round dehydrator first take a tray off the dehydrator base, load it and then return it to the base and turn on the heat. This eliminates the fear of spilling something onto the base and damaging the workings of the unit.

Always place wet meat or fish jerky in a single layer. Pieces should lie flat with no overlapping on dehydrator trays. Do not overload trays. On a round tray that is 15½ inches across, I generally fit ¾ to one pound of strips cut ¼-inch thick.

During the drying process, you may need to rotate the trays from top to bottom and turn each piece of food every few hours to get a better dried product, depending on the type of dehydrator and its air flow pattern.

SMOKERS

Smoking meat and fish as a method of preservation goes back to the time when people first used fire. Sumerians did it, Native Americans did it and today we still do it. Dry smoky air removes water, adds flavor and has a preservative effect. Smoking and drying occur simultaneously. According to Dr. Art Maurer, when smoke accumulates on the surface of jerky, the smoke's slight anti-oxidant effect retards the development of rancidity and bacterial growth.

The most commonly used woods to produce smoke include hickory, alder, mesquite, sugar maple, birch, willow, apple, cherry, peach, pecan and beech in various size chunks, chips, sawdust and shavings. Other items used include coffee husks, corn cobs, sugar cane pulp, coconut husks, rice straw, grape vines, nut hulls, fruit pits, green willow and juniper branches, aspen and oak leaves. In some parts of the world, even dried cow dung. Sometimes fruit peels and fresh and dried herbs are tossed on the hot coals to add more flavor and interest.

Various woods produce smoke that can change the color and taste of jerky. Willie Cambern owns a class-act butcher shop called Willie's Grocery and Locker in the town of Fountain, Minnesota. He makes great jerky in his smokehouse. He combines equal portions of hickory and maple chips. Hickory alone, he says, is too bitter and produces a dark brown or black jerky. Maple imparts a sweeter taste and gives his jerky a redder color.

Smoked jerky has a shinier, smoother appearance than jerky that's just dried. This coating helps seal in natural flavors.

All smokers are metal containers with a heat source—briquettes, electricity or gas—on the bottom. Chips, shavings, chunks or sawdust smolder over the heat source. The jerky to be smoked is placed on a rack. The smoke swirls up and around all surfaces of the meat or fish strips placed above it. A pan of water sits between the smoke and the strips.

In electric smokers, there's an element on the bottom that supplies a constant flow of heat to a bed of lava rocks. Wet wood items are placed on top of the hot lava rocks. A water pan is placed above the chips. Meat or fish strips go on racks stacked above the chips. About an hour after an electric smoker starts, the wood chips turn to ash. To smoke foods longer than one hour, remove the racks and pan and repeat the process.

Smokers can be purchased for $30 and up. Grills made of heavy metal may cost more, but they last longer. Smokers have round bottoms that help distribute heat evenly.

My father-in-law Vince Deden is the keeper of the jerky smoking secrets in our family. He makes terrific smoked venison jerky, so I turned to him to learn more about the process. Smoking is a ritual, really, that taps into the evolution of food preservation. There's a maleness about it, too. Women historically did the brining and men kept the smokehouse fires smoldering.

The attraction of smoked foods is instinctive, if not genetic, explaining why so many jerky recipes have liquid smoke in common. Some call for as little as a teaspoon; others call for as much as half a cup. Too much liquid smoke dominates the flavor of jerky.

When Vince loaned me a smoker (since then I've purchased my own), he also shared his techniques and recipes. Even though he was smoking his venison jerky as long as 8 hours, he was also adding liquid smoke to his marinade, which we both now know was overkill. Once I caught on to how Vince did his smoking, I began experimenting with using my electric food dryer in conjunction with a smoker. First, I dry off the surface moisture in the dehydrator, which takes 1 to 2 hours. (Smoke adheres to a dry surface better than a wet one. I learned this when I visited the Pacific Northwest. Larry Fountain of Larry's Smokehouse near Seattle told me that smoke will not penetrate a wet surface.) Secondly, I put the strips in the smoker for another hour, then return the jerky to the dehydrator to finish drying. This sequence strikes me as the most efficient. Vince agrees, because it cut his jerky-making time in half.

17

I have used a smoker with meat or fish strips and ground products including soy protein, formed into strips. How long it takes to smoke foods depends on what foods are being made into jerky, the size of the strips, how much liquid is in the wet jerky, if it contains fat, the amount of smoke and how fast it moves, the humidity of the outside air and the temperature inside the smoker.

USING A SMOKER TO MAKE JERKY
■ **Always use smokers outside.**
■ Keep out of reach of children.
■ Pay attention to the wind. If it's too strong, wait until the air calms down.
You'll need:
    ■ long-handled tongs
    ■ oven mitts that can get dirty
    ■ charcoal briquettes
    ■ charcoal lighter—choose an odorless fire starter, an electric starter or a charcoal chimney, (which eliminate the need for a fluid starter)
    ■ smoke producers such as chips, saw dust or shavings (see list on page 16)
    ■ 3-pound coffee can container to transport water to the smoker pan

One hour before beginning the smoking process, soak ½ cup hickory and ½ cup mesquite chips or sawdust in 1 cup water. Larger pieces may require a longer soaking time. Wet wood produces more smoke and smolders better than when it's dry. Fresh, green wood chips can be dried in a dehydrator to use for smoking.

Fill an empty coffee can full of charcoal briquettes. About one hour before the smoking process begins, cover briquettes with lighter. Light and leave uncovered until the coals are hot and glow with a white ash.

Once coals are hot, use oven mitts to hold the coffee can. Empty the hot coals onto the smoker's bottom. Use tongs to spread coals away from bottom center air hole. The hole needs to be kept open in order for air to enter. Add about a dozen new, unlit briquettes to the hot coals. Spread the soaked chips evenly over the hot coals using the long-handled tongs. Next, suspend a center pan or pot that holds water over the coals and chips. Make sure it is put securely in place so it does not tip and spill. Carefully pour in water. If water hits the hot coals it produces an ash that may get on the surface of the jerky. The water

18

creates steam that helps smoke and cook the jerky. Next place the drying rack or grill securely on top of the water pan. Place wet jerky on the drying rack in single layer, making sure pieces do not overlap. Leave space between each jerky strip to allow smoke to circulate around all surfaces. Put the top on smoker and leave for one hour. Each time the lid is lifted off the smoker, smoke escapes and the process will take longer. If the smoker is not producing enough smoke and the fire is dying out, check the air holes and open the vents more. Additional oxygen will get the fire going. If the temperature gets too hot, close the vents or add cold water to the pan.

Be careful, because both the outside and the inside of the smoker can get very hot during this process.

When smoking jerky for a longer time, every hour remove smoker top, drying rack, pan of water and add another dozen briquettes and another cup of soaked chips or sawdust. Each time, stir charcoal with tongs and spread around evenly to keep the fire hot. When using a smoker as the only method of drying, it may take 6 to 12 hours of continuous smoking to dry jerky.

When using a commercial smoker for the first time, read and follow the manufacturer's directions. Each smoker has its own quirks. Some smokers have several racks and you can change their positions. Some manufacturers may suggest turning the drying jerky during the smoking process. Experimenting with the smoker is very important.

JURY-RIGGED SMOKERS

I've seen plans for making smokers out of steel drums, garbage cans, sheet metal and washtubs. A homemade smoker can be as sophisticated as building a brick smokehouse. A serious look into a pantry or cupboard may turn up an extra pan that can be used to hold smoldering coals, and non-combustible racks or poles to suspend food. A fair amount of creativity and patience can produce some wonderfully tasty and inexpensive smoked jerky.

While working with Chef Gene Gowan, he explained how smoking can be done without a smoker. Put a very dry 3- to

19

4-inch stick of wood in the oven until the embers glow visibly. Remove it with tongs. Put it in a cake pan with the food to be smoked, cover with aluminum foil, leaving one corner open to keep the ember burning and let it sit for 10 to 20 minutes in the oven. When I tried this I had trouble babying the ember to produce smoke. Perhaps using the fireplace would be wisest.

COMMERCIAL SMOKING

Commercial smoking, both hot and cold, is done in temperature controlled smokehouses or smoke ovens. In many commercial facilities, fish and beef are smoked in separate smokers to avoid a cross taste. Hot smoking dries, cooks and flavors jerky. Cold smoking just flavors jerky.

Foods to be smoked usually have been brined or coated with a dry cure. Some brines for cold smoking call for dye to give the finished jerky a more colorful appearance.

Hot smoking includes three steps. First, the wet jerky is exposed to dry air for an hour or two to remove surface moisture. During the drying stage, a pan of cold water is put in the drying chamber to encourage more air draw. The second stage is smoking. The third stage is cooking. During this stage, temperatures can range from 150 to 250 degrees F.

Cold smoking is done at temperatures from 80 to 130 degrees F. It is primarily a way to flavor jerky rather than a method of preservation. Once smoked, cold smoked foods are always refrigerated or frozen. With lower temperatures, more moisture is left in the food. It is a slower process than hot smoking. Smoking time varies from a few hours to weeks. It is possible to produce good home hot-smoked foods, but cold smoking is time consuming and more difficult. Jerky that does not reach an internal temperature of 145 degrees F. still has the potential to develop bacteria. For safety's sake, cold smoked jerky should be put in the oven or dehydrator to finish the drying process. Cold smoking is generally best for highly salted meat or fish.

GRILL SMOKING

It is possible to use barbecue and gas grills to smoke strips of meat or fish. Barbecue is really just a long, slow process of hot-smoking meats over low-banked coals. Unlike a smoker, a grill doesn't have a pan for water. The best method to produce smoke for long periods of cooking is to place larger chunks of water-soaked chips directly on the heat source.

OVEN DRYING

Gas, electric, microwave and convection ovens can be used to make jerky, although it's more difficult to control and maintain a constant temperature under 200 degrees F. Ovens heat air, but other than the convection oven, they do not circulate it. Jerky dried in an oven varies a great deal from one type of oven to the next and has more of a cooked quality than jerky dried in a dehydrator. If the heat is too high, jerky becomes tough, has a burnt flavor, a mealy texture and is more brittle than when dried in a dehydrator.

MAKING JERKY IN AN OVEN

Marinated meat and fish strips can be drippy. By lining the oven floor with aluminum foil or by placing a cookie sheet or a cake pan on the bottom shelf, you can make clean-up easier.

FOUR OPTIONS

■ Lay marinated strips crosswise over oven or cake racks. Spray racks with oil to make clean-up easier.

■ Spear strips with shower or drapery hooks or shishkabob spears and hang from the oven bars.

■ Use a toothpick to skewer a strip. Lay the toothpick across the oven rack with the strip hanging down.

■ Put strips of cut or ground meat jerky on a cookie sheet. Turn pieces over at least once during the drying process in order for the drying air to reach both the top and bottom surfaces.

21

Turn oven to 150 to 165 degrees F. In order to maintain these temperatures, you may need to turn the oven off and on every hour or so. Oven drying may take from 4 to 24 hours, depending on the size and thickness of the pieces, temperature and the type of oven.

The downside of using an oven is the lack of air flow. To promote air circulation, prop the oven door open about 1 inch with a non-burnable item between the door and oven wall. You can try placing a low-powered fan in the door opening. When using a fan, make sure you watch this arrangement carefully so that the fan doesn't move or get too hot. When using a gas oven, be careful the pilot light isn't blown out by gusts of air if a fan is part of the plan.

MICROWAVE OVEN

Microwave ovens cook food quickly. Removing water from food is not the intended purpose of a microwave oven. Over the years, I have tried to make jerky in a microwave and I've never created a jerky that compares with what I've made in a dehydrator or smoker.

Recently, I purchased a special tray for keeping slices of bacon straight during the microwave process. I put marinated meat strips across this tray and used full power. The texture and flavor of the dried product was overcooked and crisp. If you choose to experiment with drying in a microwave, I suggest you vary the power and keep a close eye on what's happening. Oven wattage varies tremendously from one microwave to another. The microwave jerky I made became dog treats.

CONVECTION OVEN

A convection oven uses circulating air to cook food faster. If you have a convection oven or you're considering buying one to make jerky, ask the manufacturer to provide you with information on how best to use it. Expect to do some experimenting.

AIR DRYING

Air drying involves placing food in direct or indirect light where dry, warm air currents can circulate around food. The more the air moves, the faster drying is accomplished. Food pieces lying flat on a surface do not get air flow from underneath and must be turned over to dry on both sides. You'll achieve   better results when air freely circulates around, over and under food. Hot air rising from a fire penetrates and dries food placed above it. Natural drying can take days. Foods dried outdoors, must be brought in or tightly covered at night to prevent them from absorbing the night's dew.

IMPROVISING WITH JERKY

Air drying has been done for thousands of years. Our ancestors survived many lean times because they had a supply of jerky. Lewis and Clark used peeled willow sticks to skewer meat and fish strips, then hung them in bushes to dry.

Meat and fish were dried on sun-warmed rock, on screens placed high above camp fires, on cookie sheets or baking cooling racks near heat registers, on radiators, near warm refrigerator air exhaust, in rear car windows and even on flat house roof tops. Strips were strung on heavy string or fishing line or pierced with hooks, rods, wire or hangers and draped over hot, rising air. For those who heated with wood stoves, a strong hook on the wall or ceiling above the stove utilized the hot radiating air by means of a suspended baking cooling rack to hold meat or fish strips. Others placed a string or wire from the ceiling above the stove and hung strips over the wire.

For safety reasons, I don't recommend making jerky outdoors. There's no way to determine or control temperatures, and airborne dirt and insects may present more than a few problems.

FOUR

MAKING JERKY

Making jerky can be as simple as sprinkling salt and pepper onto meat or fish strips and drying them over a smoky fire. Although that's a valid way to make jerky, I would like to introduce you to a bolder dimension in flavor blending. Jerky can be like fine wine, a mingling of characteristics, some subtle, others robust.

Many of the jerky marinades you'll find here were tested in the kitchen of L'Etoile, a restaurant in Madison, Wisconsin. Chef Gene Gowan's assistance in developing and testing the jerky marinades made all the difference in their success. The staff taste tested jerkies at staff supper; they made comments and gave suggestions on how to make each jerky better. During this experience, I learned flavoring and blending techniques.

Endless combinations of ingredients can be used to add flavor and color and to alter the texture of jerky. Salt, an acid such as vinegar, a sweetener and flavorings are the most common. The most interesting aspect of developing marinades is the need to use flavorings more heavily than anticipated. Yes, the taste of foods is intensified as a result of the drying process. And yes, jerky does develop a stronger flavor as it ages. Still, the more of an ingredient you add, the better the flavor. Common sense dictates that salt and liquid smoke be used in moderation.

Jerky can be made from strips of meat and fish, from ground meats and soy protein. Making it yourself gives you control over the quality, the use of chemicals, preservatives, color and flavor enhancers. I've not included

FRESH TERIYAKI SAUCE

Fresh teriyaki sauce gives jerky a special flavor.

1 tablespoon sake
1 tablespoon mirin
1 tablespoon dark soy
    sauce
Pinch sugar

Mix ingredients together in a saucepan. Bring to a boil. Remove from heat. Add to marinade.

the use of any preservatives other than salt, liquid smoke and other salt-based flavorings. Although all marinades can be used with any red or white meat or fish, some marinades suggest one type of meat or fish.

Fish is more delicate than meat and absorbs flavor easier and dries faster. Do not dry fish with other type of meats. When making fish jerky in a dehydrator, you may want to put it outside, or behind closed doors because the fish smell may be strong and undesirable in your home. One pound of fresh meat or fish generally dries to ⅓ pound.

PRETREATING

The most popular way to add flavor is **marinating** in a seasoned liquid called a marinade. Historically, meat or fish were either soaked (or marinated) in a **brine** of concentrated seawater or a **dry cure** was rubbed directly on their surface. Brines are also referred to as wet cures or pickling.

The difference between a marinade and a dry cure is a fine line. Dry cures draw water and blood out of meat and fish. As liquid develops, dry cures become brines. Strictly speaking, a dry cure is made of all dry ingredients. Generally it consists of 2 portions salt, 1 portion sugar, with herbs and spices to add flavor. Usually 1 tablespoon of dry cure is used per pound of fresh fish or meat.

Dry cure is done by laying fish or meat strips in a single layer on a clean, flat surface. The dry cure is rubbed, pressed or pounded into the flesh carefully so it holds its shape during the drying process. Cured strips are laid one on top another in a container with a tight-fitting lid. When touring smokehouses, I asked how long a dry cure was left on and was told a minimum of three and maximum of 48 hours. Most are left on eight to 24 hours and during this time are stored in the refrigerator. Turn every eight hours to make sure all surfaces remain evenly covered. Before drying, rinse in water to eliminate some of the surface salt.

A **brine** is simply a thin marinade with a high concentration of salt. Brines are most often used with fish but can also be used with meat. A basic brine contains one part salt to eight parts water (one cup salt per two quarts water). The amount of salt varies depending on the size of pieces and the desired salt concentration in the dried product. Larger pieces require a higher salt concentration. Old-time brines are very heavy in salt—sometimes producing almost inedible results.

To determine if the salt concentration is strong enough, an uncooked egg in its shell should float in the brine. All meat and fish pieces must remain submerged in the brine. Remove egg. Often a lid or a plate is put on top to weigh pieces down, making sure no pieces reach the brine surface. Place in a cool spot. After removing the fish or meat strips from the brine, rinse with fresh water. Pat with paper toweling.

Some people prefer to brine twice. First the cleaned fish or meat is brined one hour. The brine is drained off and discarded. The fish is rinsed in fresh water. Then flavorings are added to the second brine.

Brines can be hot or cold. A hot brine penetrates the meat or fish quicker, helps tenderize and promotes faster drying. When using a hot brine, salt suds may need to be skimmed off. Hot brining is a common method for pretreating venison. Bring 2 cups water to a boil. Add ½ cup salt, ¼ cup vinegar and 1 tablespoon fresh crushed black pepper-corns and boil 5 minutes longer. The meat or fish can be brined from one day to several weeks.

Another option, a **paste,** is loosely defined as a combination of the dry cure and brine methods. This can be as simple as crushing fresh garlic, adding a little olive oil and rubbing it onto meat or fish strips.

The marinades in this book vary from being very thin to very thick and although they are often called brines, marinades, cures or pastes, for my purposes I will refer to them as marinades. If the marinade is too thick, it can be thinned by adding more liquid. Most marinades are for one pound of meat or fish unless otherwise stated.

Smoking is also considered a flavoring technique. It's been my experience that just about every jerky is enhanced by putting it in a smoky environment for 30 minutes to one hour.

The first couple of times you make jerky, it's best to work with small batches until you're thrilled with the dried product. Write notes in this book on what you liked, what you didn't like and what you'll change the next time.

DOUBLE DIP DRYING

There were a few times when I dried the jerky too crisp or too hard. When this happened, I soaked it again in a simple marinade solution for just a couple minutes, then re-dried it. Not only is this a good idea when the jerky you've dried doesn't have the texture you like, it's also a good way to add more flavor. This double dip drying technique can make a so-so jerky into a great jerky.

When making jerky, always select the leanest items possible. Flank, round and loin cuts are the most popular meats because there is less bone and fat to discard. Boneless poultry breasts are especially popular. Fish are generally skinned and filleted.

Work in a very clean environment. Wash hands. Keep hands and all surfaces clean. Don't cut corners. If at any point you want to sanitize any surfaces, simply add 1 tablespoon chlorine bleach to a quart of water.

When concocting a marinade, smell and taste and make adjustments based on your senses. The following marinades can be used with a variety of meat, fish or poultry. They can be easily doubled, tripled, etc. When creating a marinade, it's a good rule of thumb to always thoroughly mix the ingredients together and allow at least 15 minutes to blend before adding the strips or ground foods. I generally use about 1 cup of liquid for strips and ½ cup liquid with ground items. When marinade

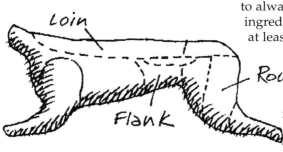

directions call for pureeing in the blender, don't blend when ingredients are hot. Cool, then blend.

When marinating any item for more than an hour, cover the container and place it in the refrigerator and stir every eight to 12 hours. Fish absorbs flavors more quickly than meat, yet can be brined for several days.

Choose containers made of glass, porcelain, earthenware or stainless steel that have lids. Avoid aluminum containers. Allow at least 15 minutes for all dry ingredients to completely dissolve in liquids before adding meat or fish. When marinating, make sure all pieces remain covered. Stir or turn the pieces at least once during the marinating process.

As I tested marinades, I started using tight-sealing plastic bags as marinating containers. Any extra air can be forced out. I like the fact that these containers take up less refrigerator space and make clean-up very easy. Whenever opening the refrigerator, pick up the bag, squeeze and move the pieces and liquid around.

When removing strips from a marinade, a colander can be a helpful tool for draining liquid away.

Marinating time varies from a few minutes to several days. The longer the marinating time, the more flavor. I marinate most ¼-inch thick foods eight to 48 hours in covered containers in the refrigerator. Some people marinate meat and fish as long as 72 hours. Thicker and bigger pieces take longer for the marinade to penetrate.

Jerky made from ground foods also benefits from overnight marinating, but can also be dried almost immediately after all the ingredients are mixed together. When marinating less than one hour, there is no need to refrigerate. In fact, I let the meat or fish and the marinade sit at room temperature for an hour, then put it in the refrigerator. It seems to me that warmer marinades penetrate surfaces faster.

A DAD STORY

My Dad was raised on a farm in the early 1900s. Every February, they butchered five 200-pound pigs. The hams and shoulders were put on long boards and Dad's job was to rub a salt cure liberally over the meat, especially around the joints. Grandma Bell made a

brine that would float a raw egg. For each 100 pounds, she combined 1 pound salt, ½ pound brown sugar and 3 ounces saltpeter. Hams were placed in the brine. A lid was placed flat down on top of the brine, allowing no air space. A clean rock was placed on top to weigh it down and the hams were left to stand 24 hours. The following day, the hams were removed and 2 pounds of salt and ½ cup black pepper were rubbed into them. After that the hams were checked every couple of days. If more salt was needed, it was rubbed on, up to 30 days. Then the salt was washed off and the hams were smoked for about 10 days using hickory wood. Once smoked, the hams were wrapped in muslin bags and hung from hooks in the granary.

SWEETENERS

Salt alone can toughen meat and fish. Sugar adds flavor and moderates the harsh taste of salt. Use light or dark brown, cane, maple or white sugar, honey or molasses.

GOOD INGREDIENTS MAKE ALL THE DIFFERENCE IN A MARINADE

SALT

Salt in one form or another is the most common jerky ingredient. Historically, seawater was evaporated for salt. Rock or mineral salt was traded along salt routes, or obtained from vegetables, wood ash and seaweed.

Salt draws water and blood from food, which induces partial drying. Salt inhibits the growth of microorganisms that cause spoilage. Salt also serves as a preservative, lengthens storage life and adds flavor. Another bonus, is that flies do not like salted meat or fish.

For most marinades, I add 1 teaspoon salt per pound of meat or fish. See the safety section on pages 7-11 for more information.

Use the purest salt you can find. Choose a good quality, food-grade sodium chloride. Coarse pickling or canning salt is a good choice because it dissolves easily in liquids. Some recipes call for kosher salt. To prevent any chemical reaction, choose the non-iodized salt if you're going to heat the marinade or brine. I don't recommend rock salt. It contains many impurities and dissolves poorly.

Soy and teriyaki sauce are the most commonly used liquid salts. I have used the Kikkoman® brand for many years. Low-salt versions are available. **Soy sauce** and **tamari** are made mainly from fermented soybeans. **Teriyaki** is made from sake, mirin, soy and sugar. **Sake** is Japan's national alcoholic beverage and is made from fermented, steamed white rice. Heating releases its rice fragrance. **Mirin** is a sweet, low-alcohol sake used for cooking.

Regarding Saltpeter and MSG

Sodium nitrate has been used to help preserve meat and fish for decades. It adds color, helps prevent spoilage and retards bacterial growth.

Nitrate is a naturally occurring mineral substance commonly known as saltpeter. During the curing process, the bacteria in the curing solution convert the nitrate to nitrite.

Many jerky recipes call for saltpeter. When I checked this out with Willie (my local butcher and main jerky maker), he gave me a sample of the saltpeter he uses to make jerky. It's pink in color to differentiate it from regular salt. Willie adds 4 ounces, which is about 2 tablespoons to 100 pounds of meat strips. Saltpeter is considered a quick cure because as soon as it's put on the meat, the color of the meat begins to change.

Some commercial salt and flavor enhancers contain monosodium glutamate (MSG). I don't use MSG or saltpeter in any of the jerky marinades in this book—which is one benefit of making it yourself. Consider instead using garlic, hickory smoke, onion or celery salts. Nitrates do not need to be used unless the drying temperature is not high enough, such as in cold smoking.

FLAVORINGS

Oil

Oil does not dry, although small amounts can be used to add flavor. I generally add one teaspoon to one tablespoon per pound of ground meat, fish or soy protein for better texture. Olive and sesame seed oils are my favorites. Many new flavored oils, such as lime, avocado, basil, olive and walnut are commercially available. If any oil beads up on the surface of the jerky during the drying process, pat it off with paper toweling.

Liquid Smoke

Liquid smoke is a very popular jerky flavoring. Hickory is the most common liquid smoke flavor. It's also available in mesquite and a hardwood flavor. In my opinion, most recipes call for too much liquid smoke and the jerky tastes of smoke and nothing else. Start with using ¼ to ½ teaspoon in a marinade that calls for one pound of meat or fish. When smoking jerky to add flavor, it's not necessary to add liquid smoke to the marinade.

In researching liquid smoke, I found that it's made in my hometown of Manitowoc, Wisconsin. During a recent visit I had the opportunity to tour the Red Arrow Company with Virgil Kreder, president. Not only does this business use a by-product of the wood industry, it uses its own by-products to power its facility.

Liquid smoke is made by burning sawdust (four to five semi loads of sawdust per day), condensing the smoke and then separating out the carcinogenic compounds.

Tar, resin and soot are removed. This means it is safer to use liquid smoke than real smoke, and it's more economical and convenient in terms of time saved and ease of application. Liquid smoke is also very effective as a natural anti-oxidant and can be used in place of BHT and BHA, both of which are synthetic. In other words, liquid smoke has a preservative, anti-bacterial and anti- oxidant effect.

Herbs and Spices

For each pound of raw meat or fish, I generally use 1 to 2 tablespoons fresh herbs, 1 to 2 teaspoons dried or ¼ to ½ teaspoon powdered. Amounts, of course, depend on the flavor strength of the herbs or spices chosen. For example, basil, bay, dill, mint, oregano, rosemary, sage, tarragon or thyme are more flavorful than chervil, chives, parsley or savory. Seeds, berries, pods, leaves and bark can be added for flavor. Consider using allspice, cardamom, cayenne, chili powder, cloves, coriander, cumin, curry, garlic, ginger, horseradish, juniper berries, mustard, nutmeg, paprika, peppercorns (black, green, pink) or pickling spices, to mention only a few.

Herbs and spices can be added whole, crushed or ground. Crush dried herbs and spices with a mortar and pestle or grind in a blender. If an ingredient has a lot of sugar or is moist, first place it in the freezer for an hour—cold foods grind more easily. Dried seasonings can be steeped like a tea, strained and added to the marinade. Make sure any large pieces are discarded because they can become tough little pieces if left on the jerky.

TENDERIZERS

Using enzymes to tenderize meat can be traced back centuries to tropical countries where raw meat was wrapped in papaya leaves prior to cooking. Papaya contains papain, pineapple contains bromelain, figs contain ficin and all tenderize meat. For one pound of meat, sprinkle about ½ teaspoon of tenderizer evenly over all surfaces. Piercing the meat with a fork helps the tenderizer penetrate deeper.

Numerous brands of commercial meat tenderizers are available. Check ingredient labels because some are especially high in sodium nitrate.

Vinegar

Vinegar was made by early Americans from strained, fermented maple sugar sap. There are many types of flavored vinegars available including cider, raspberry and tarragon. All vinegars impart a lot of flavor and serve as tenderizing agents. I generally use no more than ¼ cup per pound of meat or fish.

Alcohol

Alcohol, especially wine, brandy, sherry, whiskey and beer, add flavor and have a tenderizing effect. The alcohol content is lost during the drying process. Heating wine releases its flavor and improves the raw taste. One cup wine boiled 2 minutes concentrates the flavor and if simmered as long as 10 minutes, reduces to about ¼ cup. When reducing any alcoholic beverage, use a high-sided pan to reduce the chance of the alcohol catching fire. If it does flame, the flame will die out as soon as all the alcohol is gone. Although red wine colors meat and therefore is used with red meats and white for fish, I do not stick to this standard. Instead I use alcohol for flavor. All jerky darkens when dry. Dry (unsweet) wines are best for marinating, but sweet wines are less acidic. Wine offers a more delicate flavor than vinegar and citrus juice, although wine has more acid than apple juice.

Non-alcoholic wine-like liquids also can be used. If you don't want to use alcohol, use a mixture of vinegar and water, citrus juice and water, or apple juice mixed with a little lemon juice.

Fruits and Vegetables

The potential for using fruits and vegetables is truly an endless list. Ingredients can be in the form of fresh, frozen, canned or dried and you can use juices, pieces or purees. They can be added to a marinade raw or cooked. For example, cooked onions add a sweet taste to a marinade, or raw onions can be grated, minced, chopped or cut in rings and added. Juices include lemon, orange, pineapple, apple or tomato. Fruits and vegetables can range from slices of raw radishes to dried tomatoes. Dried foods can range from any type of pepper to grated coconut. Powders include onion, tomato, celery, garlic, lemon, papaya, lime and horseradish.

COMMERCIAL MIXES

Commercial products present an almost exhaustive list of possibilities. **Commercial spice mixes** are commonly available from grocery and sports stores, dehydrator manufacturers, specialty and spice shops, mail order, the Internet and more. Even some pet stores carry jerky spices for human as well as superb dog and cat treats. It's worth a pound or two of meat to try them. Some are absolutely wonderful and turn jerky making into a fast, easy and simple project.

Dry commercial jerky cures and seasonings are very popular. Cajun, teriyaki, mesquite, original, mountain, peppered, Hawaiian, Western, jalapeno and honey glaze are used for beef, buffalo, elk, chicken, turkey, fish and venison. Mixes generally contain salt, sugar, brown sugar and one form or another of sodium nitrate.

My friend and cohort Annie traveled to Milwaukee, Wisconsin, to visit Penzeys, Ltd. and The Spice House where she picked up several wonderful seasonings—Smoke House, Tandoori Chicken, Very Hot Cajun Style and Jamaican Style Jerk. All made great jerky. For a Penzeys catalogue, call 414-574-0277 or write P. O. Box 1448, Waukesha, Wisconsin 53187. For a catalogue from The Spice House, call 414-272-0977 or 414-272-6877 or write The Spice House, 1031 N. Old World Third St., Milwaukee, Wisconsin 53203.

One other source for jerky seasoning mixes is American Harvest. Their seasonings are made to be mixed with ground meat and come in a variety of flavors. To order from American Harvest, call 800-288-4545.

Another avenue to consider is the use of **commercial sauces** such as Tabasco®, chili, taco, salsa, Worcestershire, sweet & sour or barbecue. For a simple tomato flavor, try a bottle of ketchup or a can of tomato paste or sauce.

Commercial package mixes, such as dried onion soup, dried Italian salad dressing mix, taco mix, sloppy joe mix and various meat marinades provide yet another easy and inexpensive option. These packages generally amount to about $\frac{1}{8}$ ounce and are used with one pound of strips or ground meat. If the mix is salt-free, add 1 teaspoon salt per pound of meat.

FIVE

STRIP JERKY

Any kind of meat works in these marinade recipes. Grandpa's Venison Jerky, for example, is just as good as Grandpa's Beef Jerky or Grandpa's Buffalo Jerky. Whatever meat you use, choose lean cuts, such as flank, round and loin which have less bone and fat. Choose a flat cutting surface that's easily cleaned and get yourself a sharp knife. Use the knife to remove any excess fat, gristle, membranes and tissue. Pull off membrane divisions or parchment. L'Etoile chef Gene Gowan calls this "the silver skin." Eliminating as much fat as possible helps reduce a gamey or wild taste and helps prevent jerky from turning rancid quickly.

An electric slicer works very well, especially with frozen meat. Slicers produce uniform sized pieces. Pieces cut the same size dry in the same amount of time. It's OK to ask a butcher's help with slicing—I do. Cutting across the grain produces a jerky that's easier to break apart and chew. Cut into narrow strips ⅛- to ⅜-inch thick and 5 to 6 inches long. Thin strips dry faster. When young people are making jerky, use caution handling sharp knives or slicers.

Frozen or semi-frozen raw meat cuts more easily than meat at room temperature. In my experience, meat thawed naturally has a better flavor and texture than meat thawed in a microwaved.

Some marinades, such as Mole Jerky, can be thick as molasses. Others, such as Teriyaki Jerky, can be watery thin. Don't let consistency concern you. Thick or thin, they're all flavorful.

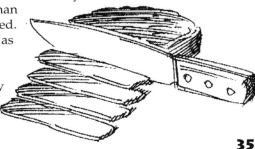

TERIYAKI JERKY

Jerky made from strips and flavored with teriyaki can be found in convenience stores throughout North America. Teriyaki is probably the most popular flavor of jerky. Making it can be as easy as opening a bottle of teriyaki sauce and pouring it over meat or fish strips. A hot pepper and 1 teaspoon horseradish and ½ teaspoon ginger will give this marinade more zing.

1 cup teriyaki sauce
1 teaspoon minced garlic
½ teaspoon salt
½ teaspoon freshly ground black pepper
½ teaspoon liquid smoke (optional)
2 pounds strips

Mix all ingredients together with the exception of strips. Allow the ingredients at least 15 minutes for flavors to blend. Add strips. Marinate at least one hour. For longer marinating time, place in the refrigerator in a covered container or in an airtight plastic bag. Remove from marinade and place in a drying environment.

MOLE JERKY

3 ounces dried New Mexican peppers or ancho chilies
1 cup tomato juice, divided
½ cup diced onion
3 tablespoons sesame seeds
2 tablespoons smooth peanut butter
2 teaspoons salt
1½ teaspoons ground cinnamon
1 teaspoon ground coriander
¼ teaspoon ground cloves
3 ounces semi-sweet chocolate, chopped coarsely
2 pounds strips

Put dried peppers in a pan, cover with water and bring to a boil. Reduce heat, simmer 30 minutes. Discard water. Add ½ cup of the tomato juice and puree. Strain to remove seeds and skin. Set aside. Combine other ingredients (except chocolate) in a pan, mix well. Boil to reduce by a fourth. Add chocolate and keep stirring until melted. Bring to a boil. Reduce again by a fourth. Cool and puree in a blender. Add pepper puree. Allow flavors to blend for 15 minutes. Marinate at least one hour. For longer marinating time, place in the refrigerator in a covered container or in an airtight plastic bag. Remove from marinade and place in a drying environment.

Mole (other than guacamole) was first explained to me as chocolate sauce. It's an Nahuatl word that's pronounced "MO-lay." Mole is a lot more than just a way to flavor meat with chocolate. Mole is quite thick, given that it's a combination of dried chiles, nuts, seeds, spices and chocolate. A true mole has a triumvirate of peppers—mullato, ancho and pasilla.

Note: Use 2 pounds of meat strips for this marinade.

GRANDPA'S VENISON JERKY

This is the family favorite. My father-in-law Vince says "Give it at least 36 hours to marinate—the longer the better." Once the venison is marinated, Vince dries it about three hours in his dehydrator. Then he puts it in his smoker for an hour or two to give it more flavor and to complete the drying process. This jerky makes good bouillon, see page 108.

¾ **cup soy sauce**
1 **tablespoon brown sugar**
1 **teaspoon liquid smoke**
1 **teaspoon salt**
½ **teaspoon minced garlic**
½ **teaspoon grated ginger**
½ **teaspoon freshly ground black pepper**
1 **pound strips**

Mix all ingredients together with the exception of strips. Allow the ingredients at least 15 minutes for flavors to blend. Add strips. Marinate at least one hour. For longer marinating time, place in the refrigerator in a covered container or in an airtight plastic bag. Remove from marinade and place in a drying environment.

BLOODY MARY JERKY

½ cup V-8® juice
½ cup vodka
3 tablespoons Worcestershire
1 teaspoon honey
1 teaspoon celery salt
½ teaspoon hot sauce
½ teaspoon grated horseradish
¼ teaspoon freshly ground black pepper
Squirt of lemon or lime juice
2 pounds strips

Mix all ingredients together with the exception of strips. Allow the ingredients at least 15 minutes for flavors to blend. Add strips. Marinate at least one hour. For longer marinating time, place in the refrigerator in a covered container or in an airtight plastic bag. Remove from marinade and place in a drying environment.

On Sunday, at noon, our friend Betty King would make herself a Bloody Mary. In her memory, we've tipped our glasses together, now we klink strips of jerky. Annie suggested we use a strip of this jerky to dunk into a Sunday Bloody Mary instead of a stick of celery. Add a fistful of 1-inch pieces of this jerky to any spaghetti sauce.

39

JORDAN'S ROWDY JERKY

Jordan Grunow is one of those creative people who live a rustic lifestyle in the Wisconsin north-woods. For his family, jerky is not a luxury item, but a staple. Jordan has a reputation among his friends as a really great cook. Everyone who tasted his jerky liked it. Sue said "more salt," Adeline said "less salt." Vince said "use stronger scotch" and the kids said "don't change a thing." This jerky is particularly wonderful made with venison and then smoked.

1 cup cheap scotch
1 tablespoon soy sauce
2 tablespoons brown sugar
1 tablespoon oil
1 teaspoon salt
½ teaspoon liquid smoke
½ teaspoon freshly ground black pepper
1 pound strips

Mix all ingredients together with the exception of strips. Allow the ingredients at least 15 minutes for flavors to blend. Add strips. Marinate at least one hour. For longer marinating time, place in the refrigerator in a covered container or in an airtight plastic bag. Remove from marinade and place in a drying environment.

BOB'S BEST JERKY

2 bottles (12 ounces each) root beer
1 tablespoon minced garlic
1 teaspoon freshly ground black pepper
1 teaspoon salt
1 teaspoon liquid smoke
Salt and pepper to sprinkle
1 pound strips

Reduce root beer to 1 cup over medium heat. Remove from heat and add remaining ingredients with the exception of meat. Allow the ingredients at least 15 minutes for flavors to blend. Add strips. Marinate at least one hour. For longer marinating time, place in the refrigerator in a covered container or in an airtight plastic bag. Remove from marinade and place in a drying environment. After putting strips in drying environment, sprinkle the top with extra salt and pepper.

Bob Zank is an award-winning marksman. Each year he spends his vacation time hunting. Over the years, he has used this marinade with deer, elk and antelope. Of all the jerkies he has made, he felt this was his best. Bob says this jerky is both sweet and tangy.

CURRY JERKY

Curry powders vary in color, smell and taste. I encourage you to choose a fresh, strong smelling curry. This marinade blends well with meat, fish or poultry.

1½ cups finely chopped onion
1 cup (8 ounces) plain, non-fat yogurt
2 tablespoons finely chopped fresh mint
1 tablespoon curry powder
1½ teaspoons salt
1 pound strips

Mix all ingredients together with the exception of strips. Allow the ingredients at least 15 minutes for flavors to blend. Add strips. Marinate at least one hour. For longer marinating time, place in the refrigerator in a covered container or in an airtight plastic bag. Remove from marinade and place in a drying environment.

CAJUN JERKY

1 cup tomato juice
2 teaspoons cayenne pepper
1½ teaspoons dried thyme
1½ teaspoons dried basil
1½ teaspoons onion powder
1 teaspoon white pepper
½ teaspoon freshly ground black pepper
½ teaspoon garlic powder
1 pound strips

This marinade will add more than a little zip to fish, poultry or meat. To make it hotter, increase the amount of cayenne and if that's not hot enough, add a teaspoon or two finely chopped jalapeno peppers.

Mix all ingredients together with the exception of strips. Allow the ingredients at least 15 minutes for flavors to blend. Add strips. Marinate at least one hour. For longer marinating time, place in the refrigerator in a covered container or in an airtight plastic bag. Remove from marinade and place in a drying environment.

BARBECUE JERKY

During the taste-testing process, the kids and the L'Etoile staff loved this one. It's very sweet and sticky, like a barbecue should be. The word barbecue comes from a Spanish word "barbacoa," the name of the green-wood lattice frame the Caribbean islanders used to hold strips of salted meat to be dried over a fire. This meat preservation technique was called "bouc," which translated into French as bou-canier, from which buccaneer was derived.

2 tablespoons brown sugar
2 tablespoons white sugar
1 tablespoon oil
¼ cup minced onion
1 cup beer
⅔ cup ketchup
2 tablespoons cider vinegar
2 tablespoons Worcestershire
2 teaspoons ground ginger
1 teaspoon salt
1 teaspoon minced garlic
1 teaspoon Dijon mustard
1 teaspoon liquid smoke
½ teaspoon freshly ground black pepper
Dash of cayenne
1 pound strips

Combine sugars, oil and onion in a hot pan. Stir. Reduce heat, cook until onions caramelize. Add beer. Simmer. Cool. Mix remaining ingredients together with the exception of strips. Allow at least 15 minutes for flavors to blend, then grind in a blender. Add strips. Marinate at least one hour. For longer marinating time, place in the refrigerator in a covered container or in an airtight plastic bag. Remove from marinade and place in a drying environment.

FRUITY JERKY

½ cup dried cranberries
2 tablespoons chopped dried papaya
1¼ cups orange juice
¼ cup chopped onion
2 tablespoons brown sugar
2 tablespoons white sugar
1 tablespoon oil
1 teaspoon salt
½ teaspoon freshly ground black pepper
1 pound strips

Rehydrate cranberries and papaya in orange juice. Cook onion and sugars over medium heat until evenly browned (caramelized). Use caution not to burn. Add remaining ingredients, except meat. Simmer for just a few minutes. Cool. Allow the ingredients at least 15 minutes for flavors to blend. Puree in a blender for about one minute. Add strips. Marinate at least one hour. For longer marinating time, place in the refrigerator in a covered container or in an airtight plastic bag. Remove from marinade and place in a drying environment.

Everybody loved this one. The idea of making a fruit jerky came from Mohamed EL-Assal. He's an extremely creative chef at The Art House Restaurant in Madison, Wisconsin. The dried papaya serves as a tenderizer as well as a flavoring agent. Various combinations of dried and/or fresh fruits can be used. Add nutmeg and cinnamon to dried plums and use when making chicken jerky. This jerky is sweet, tender and a little sticky.

RED WINE JERKY

This jerky was loved by some and not appreciated by others, proving that taste is a personal thing. Several people said it reminded them of boeuf Bourguignon. Heating wine releases and concentrates its flavor. To change this for poultry, add 1 teaspoon dried tomato powder and ½ teaspoon crushed dried rosemary.

½ cup chopped onion
1 teaspoon minced garlic
1 tablespoon oil
1 cup full-bodied dry red wine (Pinot Noir)
1 tablespoon finely chopped fresh thyme
1 teaspoon brown sugar
1 teaspoon salt
1 bay leaf, medium size
½ teaspoon freshly ground black pepper
1 pound strips

Saute onion and garlic in olive oil until lightly translucent over medium-high heat. Add wine and boil 2 minutes to cook off alcohol. Simmer. Remove from heat. Add all remaining ingredients except meat. Allow at least 15 minutes for flavors to blend and for it to cool enough to pour into the blender. Remove bay leaf. Blend and add strips. Marinate at least one hour. For longer marinating time, place in the refrigerator in a covered container or in an air-tight plastic bag. Remove from marinade and place in a drying environment.

ANTICIPATION JERKY

⅓ cup rice vinegar
⅓ cup white wine
1 tablespoon olive oil
1 tablespoon lemon juice
1 tablespoon Worcestershire
1 tablespoon finely chopped fresh basil
1 tablespoon finely chopped fresh chives
1 tablespoon finely chopped fresh oregano
1 tablespoon finely chopped fresh rosemary
1 tablespoon finely chopped fresh tarragon
2 teaspoons sugar
1 teaspoon salt
1 teaspoon minced garlic
1 teaspoon freshly ground black pepper
½ teaspoon Dijon mustard
1 pound strips

This jerky gets better and better with time. The marinade can be varied easily with fresh savory and thyme. Or add more zing with ½ teaspoon crushed red peppers and ¼ teaspoon Tabasco®. For poultry, add 2 tablespoons fresh lemon thyme. For fish, add 1 tablespoon fresh fennel and 1 tablespoon fresh chervil.

Mix all ingredients together with the exception of strips. Allow the ingredients at least 15 minutes for flavors to blend. Add strips. Marinate at least one hour. For longer marinating time, place in the refrigerator in a covered container or in an airtight plastic bag. Remove from marinade and place in a drying environment.

PETER'S BURGUNDY JERKY

Peter Beck is the photographer who shot the picture of me for the back cover. He is also an accomplished hunter. Several months after he got his first dehydrator he started drying his game. Peter says "The secret to great jerky is a well-seasoned marinade over a long time." He marinates ¼-inch thin venison strips at least three days in the refrigerator, stirring once each day. He uses this jerky in his Pasta con Carne Seca on page 119.

2 cups Burgundy wine
½ cup soy sauce
3 cloves garlic, chopped
3 tablespoons molasses
1 tablespoon olive oil
1 tablespoon coarsely cracked black pepper
1 pound strips

Mix all ingredients together with the exception of strips. Allow the ingredients at least 15 minutes for flavors to blend. Add strips. Marinate at least one hour. For longer marinating time, place in the refrigerator in a covered container or in an airtight plastic bag. Remove from marinade and place in a drying environment.

48

HOT JERKY

2 fresh jalapeno peppers (2 to 3 inches each), seeded and chopped or 1 habanero
⅓ cup soy sauce
1 teaspoon freshly ground horseradish
1 tablespoon oil
1 tablespoon rice vinegar
⅔ cup water
1 tablespoon minced garlic
1 teaspoon salt
1 teaspoon Tabasco®
½ teaspoon chili powder
½ teaspoon liquid smoke (optional)
1 pound strips

Mix all ingredients together with the exception of strips. Allow the ingredients at least 15 minutes for flavors to blend and the oil from peppers to distribute throughout the marinade before adding strips. Add strips. Marinate at least one hour. For longer marinating time, place in the refrigerator in a covered container or in an airtight plastic bag. Remove from marinade and place in a drying environment.

Taste-testers unanimously loved this one. Hot is a relative word. For some, any pepper is hot; others can add a crushed habanero pepper and still claim it's not hot enough.

The fresh chopped jalapeno pepper is what makes this jerky bite back. Depending on the type of hot pepper you use for this marinade, you may want to have something handy to drink.

SAGE JERKY

1 cup hot water
1 cup whole dried sage leaves
¼ cup sliced leeks
1 tablespoon apple juice
1 teaspoon salt
½ teaspoon coarsely ground black pepper
¼ teaspoon liquid smoke
1 pound buffalo strips
Salt

Combine water and sage and let sit at least 15 minutes for flavors to blend. This process is like steeping tea. If a stronger flavor is desired, double the amount of sage. Strain sage leaves from liquid. Add leeks, apple juice, salt, pepper and liquid smoke. Puree in the blender. Allow the ingredients at least 15 minutes for flavors to blend. Add strips. Marinate at least one hour. For longer marinating time, place in the refrigerator in a covered container or in an airtight plastic bag. Remove from marinade and place in a drying environment. Once strips are placed in a drying environment, sprinkle salt over the top.

Note: In developing marinades to dry buffalo, my goal was to not mask or overpower the natural flavor, rather to enhance it. I tried to choose ingredients similar to ones available to Native Americans, such as juniper berries, cider, maple syrup and sage. For variety, substitute dill for sage and add 4 crushed juniper berries. Try this marinade with mule deer.

TASAJO

½ cup water
½ cup cornmeal
½ tablespoon salt
2 teaspoons grated onion
1 teaspoon liquid smoke
5 crushed juniper berries
1 pound strips

Mix all ingredients together with the exception of strips. Allow the ingredients at least 15 minutes for flavors to blend. Add strips. Marinate at least one hour. When strips are removed from the marinade, they are coated with corn meal. For longer marinating time, place in the refrigerator in a covered container or in an airtight plastic bag. Remove from marinade and place in a drying environment.

When I began drying buffalo, I thought it was a good idea to combine it with corn. Then I found out tasajo (ta-SA-ho) had been made for centuries in South America. This high protein, portable food continues to provide daily sustenance. It's a whole meal like pemmican. Thin strips of raw meat were dipped in corn flour, dried in the sun and wind, then rolled up in a tight ball. The corn taste really comes through in the jerky.

CHICKEN JERKY

This is one of my favorites. Poultry is more fibrous than red meat and becomes a more brittle jerky. Thin slices dry very quickly and tear apart quite easily. For variety, substitute lemon juice for pineapple juice and add ½ teaspoon fresh ground ginger.

¼ cup pineapple juice
2 tablespoons olive oil
1 tablespoon teriyaki sauce
1 tablespoon minced onion
1 teaspoon crushed garlic
1 teaspoon salt
½ teaspoon freshly ground black pepper
1 bay leaf
1 pound chicken strips

Mix all ingredients together with the exception of strips. Allow the ingredients at least 15 minutes for flavors to blend. Add strips. Marinate at least one hour. For longer marinating time, place in the refrigerator in a covered container or in an airtight plastic bag. Remove from marinade and place in a drying environment.

JERK JERKY

¾ **cup lime juice**
½ **cup orange juice**
¼ **cup diced onion**
2 **tablespoons finely diced habanero pepper**
1 **tablespoon chopped garlic**
2 **teaspoons ground allspice**
1 **teaspoon salt**
¾ **teaspoon ground cinnamon**
¾ **teaspoon ground nutmeg**
¾ **teaspoon ground ginger**
⅛ **teaspoon ground cloves**
1 **pound beef or goat strips**

Mix all ingredients together with the exception of strips. Allow the ingredients at least 15 minutes for flavors to blend. Add strips. Marinate at least one hour. For longer marinating time, place in the refrigerator in a covered container or in an airtight plastic bag. Remove from marinade and place in a drying environment.

Jerk is becoming a popular spice in restaurants and spice shops. Jerk originated in the Caribbean and was most commonly made with goat. The allspice of Jamaica became its key ingredient. I've made jerk jerky with goat, venison and beef. If you use goat instead of beef, make sure you get rid of any fat. It's the fat that carries the goat flavor. L'Etoile chef Gene Gowan liked the way the citrus flavor came through in this jerky.

ANNIE'S TANDOORI CHICKEN JERKY

Annie Beckmann is a former newspaper food editor. We've been friends for over 25 years. Her culinary curiosity always leans toward the exotic or unusual. Once Annie got into this project, she put her dehydrator on the counter and turned her kitchen into a mixing, testing and sampling playground. Annie's Tandoori Chicken Jerky is a new spin on East Indian foods traditionally prepared in clay ovens known as tandoors.

1 cup plain nonfat yogurt
3 tablespoons Tandoori Chicken Seasoning
1 teaspoon kosher salt
1 pound chicken breast strips

Mix all ingredients together with the exception of strips. Allow the ingredients at least 15 minutes for flavors to blend. Add strips. Marinate at least one hour. For longer marinating time, place in the refrigerator in a covered container or in an airtight plastic bag. Remove from marinade and place in a drying environment. When dry, this jerky may sweat a bit once refrigerated.

Note: A dehydrator won't seal in juices like a tandoor, yet this rendition captures the spicy flavor. Annie buys her spices from Penzeys, (see page 34 for their address). She says they have the freshest and the best spice blends. Any tandoori spice blend will work. Annie recommends choosing a blend of coriander, cumin, garlic, paprika, ginger, cardamom and saffron (the ingredients in Penzeys Tandoori Chicken Seasoning).

54

KEVIN AND ANNIE'S JERKY

1 cup lite soy sauce
1 teaspoon salt
2 teaspoons hot pepper flakes
1 teaspoon sharp (hot) paprika
2 cloves garlic, minced
2 teaspoons minced fresh ginger
3 tablespoons maple syrup
1 pound strips

Mix all ingredients together with the exception of strips. Allow the ingredients at least 15 minutes for flavors to blend. Add strips. "Jerkinate" strips overnight in the refrigerator in a covered container or in an airtight plastic bag. Remove from marinade and place in a drying environment.

Maple syrup and hot pepper flakes are a terrific marriage of flavors and are the special ingredients in this marinade. They add a robust assertiveness to beef jerky, says Annie, who came up with this recipe with her precocious nephew Kevin Chumbley. As the beef strips were immersed in the marinade, Kevin asked his aunt, "How long do we have to jerkinate it, Annie?"

55

BILTONG

In Africa, jerky is often referred to as biltong. I've read references to making it from python, impala, in fact, any protein source. When taste tested, most say biltong reminds them of chicken—I've heard that before. In an attempt to duplicate a historically significant dried protein product, I chose ostrich meat. I chose apple juice and cardamom to add a sweetness to this jerky.

1 cup water
1 tablespoon salt
1 pound ostrich strips
1 cup apple juice
1 tablespoon white sugar
1 teaspoon cracked black peppercorns
1 teaspoon liquid smoke
½ teaspoon ground cardamom

Bring water and salt to a boil. Add ostrich strips. Stir. Boil strips a maximum of 3 minutes or until they turn grey-brown. Remove from heat. Drain. Mix all ingredients together with the exception of strips. Allow the ingredients at least 15 minutes for flavors to blend. Add strips. Marinate at least one hour. For longer marinating time, place in the refrigerator in a covered container or in an airtight plastic bag. Remove from marinade and place in a drying environment.

GOAT JERKY

1 can (8 ounces) sauerkraut
1 tablespoon white sugar
1 tablespoon white-wine vinegar
1 teaspoon caraway seeds
1 teaspoon coarsely ground black peppercorns
1 pound goat strips

Mix all ingredients together with the exception of strips. Allow the ingredients at least 15 minutes for flavors to blend. Add strips. Marinate at least one hour. For longer marinating time, place in the refrigerator in a covered container or in an airtight plastic bag. Remove from marinade and place in a drying environment.

Although goat is not a commonly used meat for jerky in the United States, it is used in other countries. I've been using this combination of ingredients for well over 20 years to flavor various types of meat. Taste-testers especially liked the caraway flavor.

57

LEMONY LAMB JERKY

This jerky has a tender texture. It's easy to taste both the lamb and the lemon. The lemon juice serves as a flavoring agent and tenderizer. Historically, lamb was dried by rubbing sugar over a leg of mutton, then leaving it for 24 hours. For one week, salt was rubbed on it every other day, then the meat was brined 9 days, hung to dry 3 days and finished off with cold smoking.

1 pound lamb strips
½ cup lemon juice
½ cup honey
2 tablespoons finely chopped fresh mint
1 teaspoon olive oil
1 teaspoon salt
1 teaspoon finely ground black pepper

Marinate strips in lemon juice for at least one hour. Mix all remaining ingredients together. Allow the ingredients at least 15 minutes for flavors to blend. Add strips. Marinate at least one hour. For longer marinating time, place in the refrigerator in a covered container or in an air-tight plastic bag. Remove from marinade and place in a drying environment.

HAM JERKY

¼ cup honey
¼ cup water
1 pound lean ham slices, cut ¼-inch thick
2 teaspoons Dijon mustard
2 teaspoons crushed dried pink peppercorns
2 teaspoons crushed dried green peppercorns
½ teaspoon coarsely ground black peppercorns

Heat water and add honey. Use to wet ham slice surfaces. Add mustard and pink and green peppercorns. Marinate at least one hour. For longer marinating time, place in the refrigerator in a covered container or in an airtight plastic bag. Remove from marinade and place in a drying environment. Sprinkle ground black pepper on top.

Lean ham slices can be made into jerky, but uncooked pork should never be used to make jerky. Pink peppercorns are actually berries from a bush and not a member of the pepper family. During the taste-testing process, we ate this jerky with dried pineapple. Testers agreed that this would be a great addition to pea soup.

SIX

FISH JERKY

One of the most interesting things I found while researching dried foods over the past 25 years is that almost every kind of fish has been dried throughout time and in almost every corner of the world. This is fascinating because fish is not the easiest food to preserve because it deteriorates so quickly, although coating it with salt and/or soaking it in brine overcomes the problem of perishability.

Fish have been dried in the sun and wind, hung over fires and smoked, strung on hooks and suspended from poles, laid on bamboo racks, on trays and on hot flat rocks. Big fish were filleted and deheaded. However, the collarbone just in back of the gills was left in place so the fish could be hung to dry. Medium-size pieces (1-3 pounds) air dried in three days and larger pieces took seven to 10 days.

As a landlubbed Midwestener, I'm not as familiar with preserving fish as those who live on the East and West Coasts. To compensate for my inexperience, I toured a number of fish smokehouses, researched the history of drying fish and talked to people who've dried blue gills, smelt, carp, perch, trout, salmon, red snapper, sea bass, swordfish, tuna and more.

Traditionally, dried fish was heavily salted and was not meant to be eaten as jerky. Fish made into jerky cannot be subjected to traditional salting methods because it would be inedible. Therefore, I've taken a different approach to drying fish. Fish jerky is a lightweight, high-protein snack that also can be used in cooking.

To add variety, squeeze a fresh lemon slice over a piece of fish jerky.

Fish begin to deteriorate the moment they leave water which makes it very important to work quickly when making fish jerky. Fish deteriorate faster in hot, humid weather.

Throughout the fish jerky-making process, cleanliness and sanitation are very important. Keep hands and all preparation surfaces clean. Rinse fish in fresh, clean, cool water.

Fresh fish have bright, shiny, bulging eyes, pink or red gills, smooth scales that are tight against the body, and no disagreeable odor. The flesh should be firm and spring back when touched. Frozen fish can be used but it should defrost slowly in the refrigerator. Thawed frozen fish absorbs salt and other flavorings faster than fresh fish because the cell structure is altered during the freezing process.

Select fresh, lean, firm fish, although virtually all types can be used. Fish with a low fat content of 5 percent or less are the best choice for making jerky. However, fatty fish such as salmon also can be dried. Lean, white fish such as cod, halibut and sole are the most common choices.

Most fish are filleted and deboned. As a general rule, the skin is removed, although there are times when it is left on to hold the fish together during the drying and/or smoking process. For example, when I dry smelt I do not remove the skin; and when I dry lake trout the scales are removed but the skin is left on.

Cut filleted fish into thin strips about ¼-inch thick, ½-inch wide and 3 to 4 inches long. Slashing cuts crosswise into the flesh helps flavorings penetrate deeper.

TROUT JERKY

¼ cup soy sauce
1 teaspoon minced garlic
½ teaspoon freshly ground black pepper
1 pound trout strips

Mix all ingredients together with the exception of strips. Allow the ingredients at least 15 minutes for flavors to blend. Add strips. Marinate at least one hour. For longer marinating time, place in the refrigerator in a covered container or in an airtight plastic bag. Remove from marinade and place in a drying environment.

As oil beaded up during the drying process, I patted it off. I turned the fish strips over once during the drying process.

The real test of making fish jerky is in the doing. For example, my husband recently landed a trout and we sacrificed it to the cause of jerky. I followed Paul Rauber's fish jerky suggestions from the 1996 May/June issue of Sierra Magazine. He suggested cutting long strips ½-inch thick. He marinated the fish strips in sesame oil, soy sauce and sugar. My husband, who's never really liked fish jerky, ate it off the tray—it never made it to a storage container.

SALMON SOY JERKY

Salmon is the trout's bigger cousin. Just like Trout Jerky, this jerky makes a great snack. Add even more flavor by putting it in a smoker for one hour.

½ cup soy sauce
1 tablespoon molasses
1 teaspoon liquid smoke
1 pound salmon strips

Mix all ingredients together with the exception of strips. Allow the ingredients at least 15 minutes for flavors to blend. Add strips. Marinate at least one hour. For longer marinating time, place in the refrigerator in a covered container or in an airtight plastic bag. Remove from marinade and place in a drying environment.

HONEYED SALMON JERKY

¼ **cup honey**
¼ **cup rum**
1 tablespoon lemon juice
5 whole cloves
5 crushed peppercorns
5 allspice berries
1 bay leaf
1 teaspoon salt
1 pound salmon strips

Mix all ingredients together with the exception of strips. Allow the ingredients at least 15 minutes for flavors to blend. Add strips. Marinate at least one hour. For longer marinating time, place in the refrigerator in a covered container or in an airtight plastic bag. Remove from marinade and place in a drying environment.

My mother-in-law Adeline made this jerky for us to try. We all agreed it tasted really good. Our sampling discussion focused on how useful it would be to have on hand a year's supply of dried fish. Plus, it doesn't take very much fish jerky in a recipe to produce a lot of flavor. Adeline made the Salmon Jerky Loafettes on page 128-129 with this jerky.

65

SWEET COD JERKY

My first attempt at making cod jerky was to use a lot of salt and sugar. Although heavily salted fish would be great for long-term storage, the salt made it too strong to be eaten as jerky. I added more flavor to this jerky by smoking it for two hours. It was as good as any fish jerky any of us have had anywhere.

½ **cup maple syrup**
1 **teaspoon salt**
1 **teaspoon liquid smoke**
½ **teaspoon freshly ground black pepper**
10 **crushed juniper berries**
1 **pound cod strips**

Mix all ingredients together with the exception of strips. Allow the ingredients at least 15 minutes for flavors to blend. Add strips. Marinate at least one hour. For longer marinating time, place in the refrigerator in a covered container or in an airtight plastic bag. Remove from marinade and place in a drying environment.

TERIYAKI TUNA JERKY

¼ cup teriyaki sauce
2 tablespoons water
2 tablespoons brown sugar
1 teaspoon grated fresh ginger
1 teaspoon salt
½ teaspoon minced garlic
¼ teaspoon dried tarragon
1 pound tuna strips

Mix all ingredients together with the exception of strips. Allow the ingredients at least 15 minutes for flavors to blend. Add strips. Marinate at least one hour. For longer marinating time, place in the refrigerator in a covered container or in an airtight plastic bag. Remove from marinade and place in a drying environment.

Raw tuna is not only lean, but also expensive. I really don't know how anyone could mess up a batch of tuna jerky, because raw tuna is a perfect medium for absorbing flavor. This jerky was a delicious surprise.

CAJUN CATFISH JERKY

While at the fish shop buying supplies for testing these marinades, the fishmongers behind the counter encouraged me to make a Cajun catfish jerky. It's an oily fish, so make sure it is completely dry and any excess oil is patted off.

½ cup tomato sauce
1 tablespoon grated onion
1½ teaspoons cayenne pepper
1½ teaspoons dried thyme
1½ teaspoons dried basil
1 teaspoon white pepper
1 teaspoon salt
½ teaspoon freshly ground black pepper
½ teaspoon minced garlic
½ teaspoon liquid smoke
1 pound skinned catfish strips

Mix all ingredients together with the exception of strips. Allow the ingredients at least 15 minutes for flavors to blend. Add strips. Marinate at least one hour. For longer marinating time, place in the refrigerator in a covered container or in an airtight plastic bag. Remove from marinade and place in a drying environment.

SEEDY FISH JERKY

¼ cup brown sugar
¼ cup soy sauce
1 teaspoon minced garlic
1 teaspoon salt
½ teaspoon grated fresh ginger
¼ cup white sesame seeds
1 pound fish strips, cut in 1-inch pieces or 1 pound cleaned smelt

Mix all ingredients together with the exception of strips. Allow the ingredients at least 15 minutes for flavors to blend. Add strips. Marinate at least one hour. For longer marinating time place in the refrigerator in a covered container or in an airtight plastic bag. Remove from marinade and place in a drying environment. When drying in a dehydrator, to minimize seeds from falling through the trays, place a roll-up sheet under the mesh sheet.

When using small pan fish such as lake perch or bluegill, leave the scaled skin on. When using smelt, cut the heads and tails off, then slit down the middle. Rinse with clean, cold water and use your thumbs to pinch the spine and pull it out. Rinse and drain before marinating. I added more flavor to the smelt by smoking it one hour.

69

SPICY HALIBUT JERKY

My memories of halibut go back to when I was a kid. On Fridays, meat was off limits and fish was on every menu. When I would eat dinner with my friend Margaret Dalton's family, she always referred to halibut as "the Holy fish." This holy fish makes a pretty darn tasty dried fish jerky.

1 cup onion rings, thinly sliced
½ cup orange juice
1 tablespoon finely minced jalapeno pepper
1 tablespoon soy sauce
1 tablespoon minced garlic
1 tablespoon sugar
1 teaspoon salt
1 teaspoon fresh grated ginger root
¼ teaspoon freshly ground black pepper
1 pound halibut strips

Separate onions into individual rings. Mix all ingredients together with the exception of strips. Allow the ingredients at least 15 minutes for flavors to blend. Add strips. Marinate at least one hour. For longer marinating time, place in the refrigerator in a covered container or in an air-tight plastic bag. Remove from marinade and place in a drying environment.

SOLEFUL JERKY

¼ cup freshly squeezed lemon juice
1 teaspoon Dijon mustard
1 teaspoon salt
1 teaspoon dried dill
1 teaspoon minced garlic
1 teaspoon white sugar
¼ teaspoon freshly ground black pepper
1 pound sole strips

Mix all ingredients together with the exception of strips. Allow the ingredients at least 15 minutes for flavors to blend. Add strips. Marinate at least one hour. For longer marinating time, place in the refrigerator in a covered container or in an airtight plastic bag. Remove from marinade and place in a drying environment.

After Holy Jerky, what could be better than Soleful Jerky? This is a good choice for someone who's never tried fish jerky. It's mild, yet very flavorful. Vary the flavor of the marinade by using other types of juice.

SEVEN

GROUND MEAT JERKY

Jerky made from ground meat has become very popular in the past few years. Commercially, ground meat jerkies are extruded and often referred to as textured jerky. They're easy to make and taste great. It's cheaper than making jerky out of strips, dries faster than strip jerky and is easier to chew. Ground beef, venison, turkey and chicken are the most popular ground meats used, although this is by no means a comprehensive list of choices. Consider using other wild and domesticated meats, such as moose, antelope, lamb, goat or buffalo. Any kind of ground meat works in these marinade recipes.

Choose lean ground meat. I generally select meat that is at least 90 percent lean. If meat contains fat, or if oil has been added to flavor the marinade, it may need to be patted away with paper toweling during the drying process. Ground meat is mixed with various spices, flavorings, salt and sweeteners. Another plus for making this type of jerky is that no marinade is wasted—it's all absorbed during the marinating process. It's always a good idea to let the marinades sit at least 15 minutes to allow flavors to blend before adding ground meats to them.

When grinding your own meat, first remove as much fat, bone, gristle, membrane and skin. It's important to keep all

73

According to Minnesota deer hunter John Kvasnicka, each year about 8 million pounds of venison are processed in his state alone. It's estimated that half is made into venison jerky or sausage. The main ingredient in venison sausage is pork.

When commercial processors make venison jerky, it's called "jerky, restructured," and contains pork, sodium nitrate and various seasonings. Venison processing averages $90 to $120 for a deer. It often takes several months for orders to be filled.

utensils and grinding equipment clean. When working with ground meat, there are more surfaces to attract bacteria than with strips.

Raw ground meat isn't as sticky to handle when it's cold. For easier mixing and shaping, occasionally moisten hands with water. I generally use a fork to stir the marinade and ground meat together. Longer mixing time helps ground meat hold together better. This may prove to be a helpful piece of information if you do not have access to an extruding device.

After the ground meat is flavored, it can be uniformly shaped into ⅛- to ¼-inch thick strips or round sticks. To dry, use a dehydrator or place on a cookie sheet in the oven. When dried on a cookie sheet, jerky pieces need to be turned over at least once so air can effectively reach both sides. When smoking ground meat jerky, first dry it long enough in an oven or a dehydrator so that it can hold its shape before putting it in a smoker. Generally one pound makes 10 to 12 jerky strips that are ¾-inch wide and 5 to 6 inches long.

If you do use a microwave to thaw frozen ground meats (which I don't recommend), make sure you break up any clumps in order for the marinade to penetrate all surfaces.

A PAIN IN THE TOKHES

Every August, I pack my portable display booth into my van along with 20 pounds of jerky, several gallon bags of dried apples and dried bananas and enough applesauce fruit roll-up to satisfy every hungry kid who walks past me in the Agriculture-Horticulture Building at the Minnesota State Fair. I know that tasting dried foods, especially jerky, is the quickest way for a fair-goer to embrace food drying. Over 12 challenging, 14-hour days each year, I answer thousands and thousands of food drying questions—most of which have to do with making jerky.

One day, while demonstrating a jerky gun for an enthusiastic crowd, I heard giggles, then a couple of guffaws.

"Why are you laughing?" I asked with my loaded jerky gun in hand. Standing in front of me was a young athletic couple with wholesome smiles. "Making jerky at our house is a real pain in the tokhes," the woman said. The man just kept laughing. "We like ground beef jerky the best," she continued. "We shape the seasoned ground meat into a ball about the size of a softball, put waxed paper on top of a cutting board, plunk the meat on it, put another piece of waxed paper on top of the meat and another cutting board on top of that." The man was still laughing.

"And then he plunks his posterior down on it to flatten it," she said. "That's why we've called jerky-making a pain in the tokhes." Through the smile attached to a good memory, they agreed a jerky gun would save them a lot of muss and fuss, so they bought one. "But it won't be as much fun," the woman said as they disappeared into the sea of fair-goers.

SHAPING OPTIONS

There are several handy new products that extrude ground meat into uniform shapes and sizes. With names like "jerky gun" or "jerky shooter," they resemble caulk guns or cake decorators. The gun barrel is filled with the ground meat mixture. When the trigger is pulled back, the wet mixture is extruded in uniformly shaped pieces. Some of these products have extruder nozzles in several shapes to make strips or sticks.

Another option is the Jerky Press™. It is two U-shaped metal forms that are pressed together. To use, first shape ground meat mixture into 1-inch balls. Place one half of the plastic liner on the bottom U-shaped part of the jerky press and set the meatball on top of it. Fold the other half of the plastic liner over the ball. With the top part of the jerky press, push down to flatten the meat and move the metal form back and forth to even out the ground meat and make strips about ⅛-inch thick. Remove the press and plastic liner, then carefully pick up the flattened meat mixture and place it in a drying environment.

If you don't have a gadget to help you form the meat mixture, you can simply use your hands to shape the mixture into 1-inch balls. Place the ball on top of a piece of plastic wrap or waxed paper and cover the top with another piece of wrap or paper. Use a rolling pin to flatten the meat ball into ⅛- to ¼-inch rounds no larger than 2 inches across. If your hands are wet and the mixture is cold, the meat is easier to handle.

If you have roll-up sheets with your dehydrator, place the ground meat mixture on one of these sheets. The roll-up sheet I use is round, 15½-inches diameter with a 2-inch hole in the middle. One of these roll-up sheets will hold a one-pound batch. When using a smaller dehydrator, you may need more than one roll-up sheet. Spoon the wet jerky mixture onto the sheet. Use a large spoon to spread and flatten the mixture evenly. Or use a greased rolling pin or the palm of your hand to flatten it. Do your best to get the mixture the same thickness. Place the meat-filled sheet on a dehydrator tray and dry it for about 1 hour. Using a pizza cutter or a serrated knife, make indentations or cut lines 1 to 1½ inches apart making the meat into strips. Return the tray to the dehydrator and dry another hour or until the strips can be broken apart at the cut lines. Remove the jerky strips from the roll-up sheets and place them on a dehydrator or smoker tray and continue the drying process. Removing the ground meat strips from the roll-up sheets allows the air to move more easily around the jerky on a drying tray than on a solid roll-up sheet.

If you don't have roll-up sheets you can use plastic wrap or waxed paper. Cut the paper the same size as the drying tray. This is more work and the meat has to be watched to make sure that any fat coming from it is patted away to minimize dripping. With some dehydrators, hot drippy fat could hit the heating element. Be aware that this could be a recipe for a fire.

TERIYAKI JERKY

Ground meat jerky is softer and easier to chew than strip jerky. It's a good choice when making ground meat jerky the first time. Teriyaki also works very well for venison, fish and poultry. To vary the ingredients, add 1 tablespoon brown sugar or 1 teaspoon finely grated fresh ginger.

½ cup teriyaki sauce
1 tablespoon olive oil
1 teaspoon minced garlic
1 teaspoon salt
1 teaspoon coarsely ground black pepper
½ teaspoon liquid smoke
1 pound ground meat

Mix all ingredients together with the exception of ground meat. Allow the ingredients at least 15 minutes for flavors to blend. Add ground meat. Marinate at least one hour. For longer marinating time, place in the refrigerator in a covered container or in an airtight plastic bag. Remove from marinade container. Form into shapes and place in a drying environment.

SOY SAUCE JERKY

½ cup soy sauce
1 tablespoon oil
1 tablespoon brown sugar
1 teaspoon minced garlic
½ teaspoon fresh grated ginger
½ teaspoon freshly ground black pepper
1 pound ground meat

Mix all ingredients together with the exception of ground meat. Allow the ingredients at least 15 minutes for flavors to blend. Add ground meat. Marinate at least one hour. For longer marinating time, place in the refrigerator in a covered container or in an airtight plastic bag. Remove from marinade container. Form into shapes and place in a drying environment.

For those who like a salty, flavorful jerky, try this one. Testers agreed that spending a Sunday afternoon watching a sporting event with a piece of this jerky in one hand and a cold beverage in another sounded like a good time.

SPICY TOMATO SOY JERKY

Betsy Oman, fellow dehydrator enthusiast, has made her share of ground meat jerky. During one of our conversations she commented that tomato sauce absorbs fat in ground meat jerky. All taste-testers liked this jerky. Try this with ground venison.

½ cup tomato sauce
3 tablespoons soy sauce
2 tablespoons Worcestershire
1 tablespoon white-wine vinegar
1 tablespoon brown sugar
1 teaspoon finely chopped onion
1 teaspoon salt
1 teaspoon garlic powder
1 teaspoon freshly ground black pepper
1 teaspoon grated fresh horseradish
½ teaspoon Tabasco®
½ teaspoon liquid smoke
1 pound ground meat

Mix all ingredients together with the exception of ground meat. Allow the ingredients at least 15 minutes for flavors to blend. Add ground meat. Marinate at least one hour. For longer marinating time, place in the refrigerator in a covered container or in an airtight plastic bag. Remove from marinade container. Form into shapes and place in a drying environment.

CHEESIE JERKY

¾ cup beer
1 cup grated fat-free Parmesan cheese
2 tablespoons soy sauce
1 tablespoon oil
1 teaspoon minced garlic
1 teaspoon dried basil
½ teaspoon salt
½ teaspoon freshly ground black pepper
½ teaspoon liquid smoke
1 pound ground meat

Regular cheese is too oily to add to jerky but with the new fat-free cheeses, you can have a cheese flavor without oil. For a cheesie, Italian jerky, add 2 teaspoons crushed dried tomato pieces and 1 teaspoon dried oregano or basil.

Mix beer and Parmesan cheese together. Add all other ingredients with the exception of ground meat. Allow the ingredients at least 15 minutes for flavors to blend. Add ground meat. Marinate at least one hour. For longer marinating time, place in the refrigerator in a covered container or in an airtight plastic bag. Remove from marinade container. Form into shapes and place in a drying environment.

TIPSY JERKY

How about taking a bag
full of this jerky to an
office party? The alcohol
flavor survives, but the
alcohol content is
lost, alas.

½ cup vodka
¼ cup V-8® juice
¼ cup Worcestershire
1 teaspoon white sugar
1 teaspoon celery salt
½ teaspoon hot sauce
¼ teaspoon horseradish
¼ teaspoon freshly ground black pepper
Squirt of lemon or lime juice
¼ teaspoon liquid smoke (optional)
1 pound ground meat

Mix all ingredients together with the exception of ground meat. Allow the ingredients at least
15 minutes for flavors to blend. Add ground meat. Marinate at least one hour. For longer
marinating time, place in the refrigerator in a covered container or in an airtight plastic bag.
Remove from marinade container. Form into shapes and place in a drying environment.

EASY MEXICAN JERKY

1 package (1.5 ounces) taco mix
½ cup salsa
¼ cup water
1 teaspoon salt
½ teaspoon liquid smoke
1 pound ground meat

Mix all ingredients together with the exception of ground meat. Place in a blender and puree.
Allow the ingredients at least 15 minutes for flavors to blend. Add ground meat. Marinate at
least one hour. For longer marinating time, place in the refrigerator in a covered container or
in an airtight plastic bag. Remove from marinade container. Form into shapes and place in a
drying environment.

*Making jerky can be as
simple as mixing ground
meat, salsa and a
commercial taco
seasoning mix. Consider
trying this with other
packaged seasoning mixes
such as fajita, jerk,
mesquite, onion or Cajun.
Add more spice with
1 teaspoon chili powder,
1 teaspoon finely chopped
hot peppers and a splash
of Tabasco®.*

GENE'S MEXICAN JERKY

L'Etoile chef Gene Gowan is the creator of this jerky. Taste-testers gave this the thumbs up the very first time around.

½ cup tomato sauce
½ cup finely chopped onion
¼ cup chili powder
1 tablespoon oil
2 teaspoons dried oregano
1 teaspoon salt
1 teaspoon cumin
½ teaspoon garlic powder
½ teaspoon cayenne pepper
1 pound ground meat

Mix all ingredients together with the exception of ground meat. Allow the ingredients at least 15 minutes for flavors to blend. Add ground meat. Marinate at least one hour. For longer marinating time, place in the refrigerator in a covered container or in an airtight plastic bag. Remove from marinade container. Form into shapes and place in a drying environment.

MARY'S WHISKEY JERKY

2 cups whiskey
1 tablespoon soy sauce
1 tablespoon brown sugar
1 teaspoon oil
1 teaspoon salt
1 teaspoon liquid smoke
1 teaspoon minced garlic
½ teaspoon crushed black peppercorns
1 pound ground meat

Sister Mary Newcomb said, "What could be better? Booze and a hunk of meat." Use any type of wild meat and vary the booze. Try rum, scotch or brandy, or make your own combination.

Reduce whiskey to ½ cup in a pan with high sides to prevent the fumes from flaming. Be careful. If a flame does appear, it subsides when the alcohol is gone. Add remaining ingredients to the whiskey with the exception of ground meat. Allow the ingredients at least 15 minutes for flavors to blend. Add ground meat. Marinate at least one hour. For longer marinating time, place in the refrigerator in a covered container or in an airtight plastic bag. Remove from marinade container. Form into shapes and place in a drying environment.

GEHRKE JERKY

This is a sweet barbecue style jerky. Barbecue sauces often have a regional flare: Coca-Cola® is added in the South, Coors® beer in the Rocky Mountains, maple syrup in the upper Midwest and hot peppers in the Southwest. Commercial sauces can be used straight from the bottle or doctored up with chili and cayenne powder. It's called Gehrke Jerky because I was making it the day Butch Gehrke exited this world.

¼ cup minced onion
1 tablespoon butter
½ cup beer
⅓ cup ketchup
2 tablespoons brown sugar
1 tablespoon salt
1 teaspoon minced garlic
½ teaspoon liquid smoke
½ teaspoon Dijon mustard
½ teaspoon freshly ground black pepper
1 pound ground meat

Saute onions until they turn light brown in butter. Add beer and grind in blender. Add other ingredients, except meat. Allow the ingredients at least 15 minutes for flavors to blend. Add ground meat. Marinate at least one hour. For longer marinating time, place in the refrigerator in a covered container or in an airtight plastic bag. Remove from marinade container. Form into shapes and place in a drying environment.

RED WINE JERKY

1 cup red wine (Pinot Noir)
½ cup chopped onion
1 tablespoon olive oil
2 teaspoons brown sugar
1 teaspoon salt
1 tablespoon chopped fresh basil
1 teaspoon minced garlic
½ teaspoon freshly ground black pepper
¼ teaspoon liquid smoke
1 pound ground meat

My daughter Sally emptied a bag of this jerky in no time flat. She gave it an A plus. Sal suggested adding 1 tablespoon lemon juice and ½ teaspoon freshly grated ginger for variety.

In a saucepan over medium-high heat, reduce wine to ½ cup. In a skillet, saute onion in olive oil until lightly browned over medium-high heat. Add reduced wine and allow it to heat until it just begins to boil. Remove from heat. Add remaining ingredients except meat. Allow the ingredients at least 15 minutes for flavors to blend. Allow to cool enough to pour into blender. Blend and add to meat. Marinate at least one hour. For longer marinating time, place in the refrigerator in a covered container or in an airtight plastic bag. Remove from marinade container. Form into shapes and place in a drying environment.

HERB JERKY

Although this marinade contains mainly dried herbs, feel free to substitute finely chopped fresh herbs. To add more flavor, add ½ teaspoon crushed red peppers and ¼ teaspoon Tabasco®.

⅓ cup white wine (Riesling)
1 tablespoon olive oil
1 tablespoon lemon juice
1 tablespoon Worcestershire
1 tablespoon grated onion
1 tablespoon honey
1 teaspoon salt
1 teaspoon dried basil
1 teaspoon dried oregano
1 teaspoon minced garlic
1 teaspoon freshly ground black pepper
½ teaspoon crushed dried rosemary
1 pound ground meat

Mix all ingredients together with the exception of ground meat. Allow the ingredients at least 15 minutes for flavors to blend. Add ground meat. Marinate at least one hour. For longer marinating time, place in the refrigerator in a covered container or in an airtight plastic bag. Remove from marinade container. Form into shapes and place in a drying environment.

ONION JERKY

2 cups finely chopped onion
2 tablespoons brown sugar
2 tablespoons teriyaki sauce
1 teaspoon olive oil
1 teaspoon minced garlic
1 teaspoon salt
¼ cup grated raw onion
¼ teaspoon freshly ground black pepper
1 pound ground meat

Place onions in a saute pan over high heat. Add sugar and caramelize. Stir often to avoid burning. Cook until onions turn a rich caramel color. Remove from heat. Add all other ingredients, except meat. Allow the ingredients at least 15 minutes for flavors to blend. Add ground meat. Marinate at least one hour. For longer marinating time, place in the refrigerator in a covered container or in an airtight plastic bag. Remove from marinade container. Form into shapes and place in a drying environment.

The texture of this ground meat jerky is very similar to strip jerky because the onion pieces add texture. In fact, taste-testers couldn't tell it was made from ground meat. If you don't want to chop onions, buy a 2-ounce package dried onion soup mix, mix with water, 2 tablespoons teriyaki sauce and 1 pound ground meat.

HOT JERKY

For those who want their top lip to sweat, substitute a habanero for the jalapeno pepper. This is a good marinade to use with venison.

⅓ cup teriyaki sauce
2 tablespoons seeded and finely chopped jalapeno peppers
1 tablespoon olive oil
1 tablespoon minced garlic
2 teaspoons brown sugar
2 teaspoons freshly ground black pepper
1 teaspoon fresh ground horseradish
1 teaspoon salt
½ teaspoon paprika
½ teaspoon chili powder
¼ teaspoon Tabasco
1 pound ground meat

Mix all ingredients together with the exception of ground meat. Allow the ingredients at least 15 minutes for flavors to blend. Add ground meat. Marinate at least one hour. For longer marinating time, place in the refrigerator in a covered container or in an airtight plastic bag. Remove from marinade container. Form into shapes and place in a drying environment.

TURKEY JERKY

2 tablespoons lemon juice
2 tablespoons freshly grated onion
2 tablespoons teriyaki sauce
1 tablespoon white sugar
1 tablespoon olive oil
1 tablespoon fresh grated lemon peel
2 teaspoons paprika
1 teaspoon crushed garlic
1 teaspoon salt
1 teaspoon freshly ground black pepper
½ teaspoon liquid smoke
¼ teaspoon Tabasco®
1 pound ground turkey
Salt to sprinkle

People like to say "Turkey Jerky." They laugh and then smack their lips after the first bite. Try this one, then use some of the other marinades with ground turkey. How about Hot Turkey Jerky or Herb Turkey Jerky?

Mix all ingredients together with the exception of ground meat. Allow the ingredients at least 15 minutes for flavors to blend. Add ground meat. Marinate at least one hour. For longer marinating time, place in the refrigerator in a covered container or in an airtight plastic bag. Remove from marinade container. Form into shapes and place in a drying environment. Sprinkle a little extra salt on top of the jerky while it is still moist.

LAMB JERKY

½ cup finely chopped onion
⅓ cup orange juice
2 tablespoons honey
2 tablespoons finely chopped fresh mint
1 tablespoon oil
1 teaspoon cinnamon
1 teaspoon salt
1 teaspoon fresh ground black pepper
½ teaspoon cayenne pepper
¼ teaspoon nutmeg
1 pound ground lamb

Saute onion, orange juice and honey over high heat. Cook until brown. Remove from heat. Add all ingredients except lamb. Cool. Allow the ingredients at least 15 minutes for flavors to blend. Add ground lamb. Marinate at least one hour. For longer marinating time, place in the refrigerator in a covered container or in an airtight plastic bag. Remove from marinade container. Form into shapes and place in a drying environment.

DRYING GROUND MEAT

2 tablespoons chopped onion
1 tablespoon chopped bell pepper
1 tablespoon Worcestershire
1 teaspoon minced garlic
½ teaspoon dried basil
¼ teaspoon freshly ground black pepper

Making it can be as simple as sauteing raw ground meat until browned, removing from heat, draining away any fat and drying it. Cooked ground meat can be put in a colander to rinse the oil off with hot water. Or spread the cooked meat over paper toweling and press down with your hands or a rolling pin and push oil out of the meat. Place on roll-up sheets and dry in a dehydrator or on a cookie sheet in the oven at 150 degrees. Dry until it's hard. One pound of fresh ground meat dries to 4 to 6 ounces and measures 1⅓ cup.

Although this is not really jerky, some folks want information on drying ground meat for camping and hunting trips. This flavorful, high-protein, lightweight food really pays off when you arrive at your destination and rehydrate it in a spaghetti sauce. Flavorings can be added to the ground meat during the cooking process or after it's cooked.

EIGHT

VEGETARIAN JERKY

In order to make jerky for family and friends who've decided not to eat meat, I began my quest to make tasty vegetarian jerkies. Right from the very beginning, taste-testers buoyed me by saying things like "that's great jerky!" In my opinion, not all of the vegetarian recipes are great. However, those who taste tested them enthusiastically encouraged me to include them in this collection. That said, I urge you to make a recipe, then play around with it until you get the taste and texture you like best.

The basis for most, although not all, vegetarian jerkies is soy protein. Dry soy protein is available in granular, flake and chunk varieties. Textured vegetable protein (TVP) is made from defatted, cooked soy flour. When kept cool and dry, it keeps indefinitely. One cup TVP added to 1 cup boiling water becomes 2 cups.

The product I used for the vegetarian recipes is a moist soy protein called Hearty Natural®. It contains no fat or cholesterol. It's low in sodium and high in protein, fiber and iron. It's made from purified water, soy protein, dehydrated onion, dehydrated red bell pepper, carrageenin, modified vegetable gum and caramel coloring (from corn syrup). It's available in the frozen-food section and comes wrapped in a white plastic loaf. The texture is similar to raw hamburger. There are many brands of soy protein products.

The first challenge I had trying to make jerky from soy protein was getting it to **stick together.** Soy protein needs a thickening or mucilaginous agent to hold it together during the drying process. Cooked oatmeal and/or applesauce bonds well with soy protein. Packaged instant oatmeal is the quickest and easiest to use. Simply add ¼ cup water to a 1.5-ounce instant oatmeal package (makes ½ cup) and stir until it thickens, then mix it with the other marinade ingredients.

The second challenge was to make it **flavorful.** As with other jerkies, I found I needed to add more seasonings than I initially anticipated to achieve a flavorful jerky. Salt is added for flavor and as a preservative. All of the marinades in both the strip and ground meat sections of this book can be used to add flavor to soy protein. Once all the ingredients are together, they should marinate at least 1 hour. The longer flavors are allowed to blend, the better the flavor. When marinating longer than one hour, put in a covered container and place in the refrigerator.

The third challenge was to get a jerk-like **texture**. Oil adds flavor and helps create a more meat-like texture. When drying vegetarian jerky, temperature is not as important as when making meat or fish jerky. I've found that 130 to 145 degrees F. produces the best product. Vegetarian jerky dries crisp like a cracker. If it's too crisp for your taste, soak it again in a light marinade for a few minutes

and dry it again until it's not quite as crisp. This second soaking is an opportunity to add more flavor. Still more flavor can be added by putting it in a smoky environment for one hour. Smoking is a great way to improve the flavor of any borderline jerky.

Several companies make vegetarian jerkies that are generally available at health food stores. They're made from soy (generally ground) and/or wheat (generally gluten) and flavorings.

While researching vegetarian jerkies, I came across several recipes for making it out of tofu. To experiment, I cut tofu into 1-inch by 2-inch slabs about ¼-inch thick. I soaked them in various marinades overnight. When dry, they were a bit rubbery and not as much like jerky as I wanted. However, this product would be worthwhile on a backpacking trip. With the following vegetarian jerky recipes, you'll get an idea of what's possible, then make your own concoctions. I encourage you to experiment.

VEGETARIAN JERKY

¼ cup water
1 package (1.5 ounces) instant oatmeal
1 package (1.25 ounces) dry onion soup mix
3 tablespoons water
2 tablespoons oil
1 teaspoon salt
1 teaspoon minced garlic
½ teaspoon liquid smoke
1 pound soy protein

Mix water and oatmeal together. Mix dry seasoning mix and water together. Combine oatmeal and seasoning mix. Add all remaining ingredients, except soy protein. Allow flavors to blend for at least 15 minutes. Add soy protein. Marinate at least one hour. For longer marinating time, place in the refrigerator in a covered container or in an airtight plastic bag. Remove from marinade container. Form into shapes and place in a drying environment.

This is the recipe I first shared with friends. They tasted it and asked for the recipe. Several shared it with friends and co-workers and reported they loved it. You might want to substitute a commercial dry seasoning mix, such as barbecue, teriyaki or mesquite.

EASY TACO JERKY

You can take the idea from the previous Vegetarian Jerky recipe and easily boost the flavor by adding commercial or homemade salsa. When this jerky is almost dry, put it in a smoker to add more flavor.

1 package (1.25 ounces) taco seasoning
½ cup water, divided
½ cup salsa
1 package (1.5 ounces) instant oatmeal
1 pound soy protein

Combine taco seasoning and ¼ cup of the water, stir and let sit 15 minutes. Mash salsa with a fork or grind in a blender. Mix oatmeal and remaining ¼ cup water together. Add taco mixture, salsa and oatmeal to soy protein. Marinate at least one hour. For longer marinating time, place in the refrigerator in a covered container or in an airtight plastic bag. Remove from marinade container. Form into shapes and place in a drying environment.

TERIYAKI JERKY

1 package (1.5 ounces) instant oatmeal
¼ cup water
½ cup teriyaki sauce
½ cup applesauce
2 tablespoons olive oil
1 teaspoon minced garlic
1 teaspoon salt
1 teaspoon liquid smoke
1 teaspoon freshly ground black pepper
1 pound soy protein

Not only is this a high-protein snack, use it as a cooking ingredient as well. Small pieces can be added to salads and used like bacon bits. Annie ate it as a cracker-like biscuit topped with a thin layer of cream cheese.

Mix oatmeal and water together. Add all remaining ingredients, except soy protein. Stir. Allow flavors to blend for at least 15 minutes. Add soy protein. Blend together using a fork. Marinate at least one hour. For longer marinating time, place in the refrigerator in a covered container or in an airtight plastic bag. Remove from marinade container. Place in blender and puree. What surprised me most as a result of blending was that its color changed from brown to light cream. Form into shapes and place in a drying environment. It dried very fast, had good flavor and was lighter both in color and texture.

TASTES-LIKE-MEAT JERKY

My goal in making vegetarian jerky was to come up with one that people thought was meat. My breakthrough came when I made Whiskey Jerky. In that recipe, instead of pureeing the caramelized onions, I added the cooked pieces to the marinade. The result was jerky with a texture like strip jerky. I took the same approach with this marinade. I smoked it for an hour and all testers said they couldn't tell it wasn't meat. Success!

2 cups finely chopped onion
1 tablespoon brown sugar
½ tablespoon minced garlic
1 tablespoon soy sauce
1 teaspoon freshly ground black pepper
1 teaspoon salt
1 tablespoon hot pepper or olive oil
1 tablespoon rum
1 teaspoon liquid smoke
½ cup finely grated raw onion
1 tablespoon grated raw, green bell pepper
1 package (1.5 ounces) instant oatmeal
¼ cup water
1 pound soy protein

Caramelize onions in brown sugar. When browned, add garlic. Remove from heat. Add next eight ingredients. Stir and allow flavors to blend at least 15 minutes. Mix oatmeal with water and add to soy protein. Mix flavorings and soy protein together. Marinate at least one hour. For longer marinating time, place in the refrigerator in a covered container or in an airtight plastic bag. Remove from marinade container. Form into shapes and place in a drying environment.

NINE

USING JERKY

It's simple. Just take jerky from the dry state and juice it up. Jerky becomes a flavorful ingredient in a range of delicious, interesting, sometimes even outrageous new foods.

People seem surprised when I suggest using jerky in soup or stew. I add ground meat, fish jerky or jerky strips to spaghetti sauce, casseroles and breads. I toss small jerky pieces into hash and rice, and I throw some into omelets. In other words, use jerky like commercial bacon bits. Jerky is a great substitute for prepared foods such as salami. Or use it for pizazz as a pizza topping.

Jerky is right up there when it comes to fat-free and healthy. Think about it. Only lean meats are made into jerky. Many of the meats chosen for jerky are from the wild where chemicals and hormones are not spoonfed into the soon-to-market meat. Some of the benefits of using jerky include a reduction in cooking time. There's less need for refrigeration and freezer space. It's great to take along on away-from-home adventures. It also makes a great snack. Once dried, jerky becomes more potent. That means you can use less in a recipe than when you use fresh meat or fish.

None of this is really new—jerky is a food with a rich history. Native Americans knew the value of jerky as a flavorful addition to a kettle of dried corn, squash and beans. They'd shave small pieces of jerky from a larger hunk to make what we call chipped beef. We should thank the Native Americans for pemmican, one of the earliest high-protein, portable foods. To add more flavor, dried meat and fish strips were pierced with a stick and propped over hot coals. The skewered meat and fish were turned to toast both sides.

As a rule, I use about 1 cup liquid to rehydrate ½ cup jerky. Sometimes jerky is added to dishes that already have adequate liquid without any presoaking. Wine, vegetable and fruit juices, even hard liquor can be used as rehydration liquids. When any rehydrating liquid is not absorbed, try to use it as a recipe ingredient instead of discarding it.

The smaller the pieces, the faster the rehydration time. Generally, 15 minutes for ½-inch pieces is adequate. Longer soaking produces more tender products. If rehydrating longer than one hour, soak it in the refrigerator. Warmer rehydration liquids shorten the rehydration time.

Slow cooking in a crock pot is a great way to use jerky. Jerky softens the most when cooked. One cup of dry jerky generally will swell to about 1½ cups when cooked. An option is to rehydrate it 15 minutes to one hour and then simmer until jerky softens. Depending on the size of pieces, the time can vary from just a few minutes to an hour.

Salty fish jerky is generally rehydrated in either cold water or fresh milk. Then the rehydration liquid is discarded because of its high salt content.

POWDERING JERKY

Jerky can be torn apart with your fingers or cut with a serrated knife or kitchen scissors into small pieces. I generally cut jerky into ½-inch pieces. Blend either meat or fish jerky strips or ground meat jerky in a blender. Generally 3 to 4 strips will produce ¼ to ⅓ cup powder.

Shredded jerky in a can has become a popular snack food. Powdered jerky takes shredded jerky one step further. When grinding to a powder in a blender, use only a small amount of jerky at one time. It grinds more evenly. A 1-inch wide by 5-inch long piece becomes about 1 tablespoon of jerky powder. A blender or food processor is easier to use than a cheese grater.

THE ULTIMATE TRAIL MIX

2 cups jerky, cut in ½-inch pieces
2 cups salted Beer Nuts®
1 cup dried sweet or dill pickle, cut in ¼-inch pieces
1 cup salted sunflower seeds
1 cup pumpkin seeds
1 cup dried shredded coconut
¼ cup sesame seeds (optional)

Mix together all ingredients. For short-term storage, use sealable plastic bags. For long-term storage, place in refrigerator or freezer.

Makes 6 cups.

What more could you want—jerky, beer nuts and pickles? This combination was a unanimous hit. Sweet and/or dill pickles are cut into small (¼ to ½-inch) pieces and dried until chewy. Depending on personal preferences, ingredients can be varied. Ground meat jerky is my first choice for this recipe because it's easier to chew. But again, it's your choice.

103

TRADITIONAL PEMMICAN

Jerky was ground or powdered using a special one-faced hammer called a pemmican mallet or it was pounded with rock mortar and pestles. Flavorful dried wild fruits such as strawberries, blueberries, huckleberries, raspberries, chokecherries, grapes (raisins) and plums were pounded into a chunky powder.

Native Americans living on the plains are credited with developing pemmican. It was made from a combination of powdered or finely chopped dried meat, dried berries and melted animal fat (bone marrow was preferred) mixed into a thick paste and stuffed into airtight animal skins. It's a high-protein, calorie-rich, concentrated snack food in a portable, compact form. Pemmican provided an important food source for Native Americans. It was used by the Arctic explorers Robert Perry and Admiral Richard Byrd and served as a World War I survival ration. Perry and Byrd reported that initially their men did not relish pemmican, but eventually they looked forward to eating it.

Although pemmican was mainly eaten cold as a snack, it often became a flavorful ingredient in one-pot meals. Pembina, North Dakota, by the late 1700s became the Native American marketing center for pemmican. Early in the 1800s, as the trade reached its peak, fillers and flavoring such as oatmeal, potato flour, dried vegetables and a variety of seasonings were added.

Pemmican was most often made from buffalo, venison or beef, although it has been made from moose, beaver, antelope, elk, rabbit, fish—in other words, anything available or edible. The first pemmican recipe I found began, "Cut up one elk." As you might guess, exact measurements are difficult to find. Pemmican can be made to reflect your individual taste, so experiment.

Dakota Pemmican Mallet

1½ cups powdered or shredded jerky
1 cup dried fruit
1 cup warm fat
Intestinal casings

When using intestines, for safety's sake, let the scraped and cleaned intestines sit in salted water at least 1 hour prior to stuffing. Combine jerky and fruit and pour warm fat over. Fat is warmed so it's soft and pliable before combining with jerky and dried fruit. Let sit until thickened to a paste. Stuff casings and tie off ends.

Cracked bones were boiled in water and the rich, sweet, salty butter-like fat was skimmed off to use in pemmican. Or animal fat was cut into small (1-inch) chunks, heated in a pan over a slow fire and never left to boil. Casings from animal innards (intestines or stomach linings) were scraped clean and used as vessels for storing pemmican.

MODERN PEMMICAN

Doris Mueller discovered pemmican is considered a forerunner of mincemeat.

Choose a spicy hot jerky, either strips or ground meat. Whiskey Jerky (p. 85) is a good choice. For more flavor add a pinch of ground red pepper, chopped peanuts or a touch of honey. Various dried fruits can be used such as apricots, apples, pineapple, kiwi. Add dried rose hips (vitamin C), and you've created an almost complete life-sustaining portable food.

1½ cups powdered jerky
1 cup dried fruit, chopped in ⅛-inch pieces
1 cup creamy peanut butter
Plastic wrap

Grind a few pieces of jerky at a time in the blender. Smaller pieces grind faster. Then grind dried fruits. Combine all ingredients together and mix well. Spread a 12- by 14-inch sheet of plastic wrap flat on the counter. Spoon half of the mixture onto the wrap in a log shape. Pull the wrap around the pemmican mixture to force and compress it into a log shape. If necessary, use more plastic wrap to press it into a log shape. Repeat with the other half of the mixture. Make sure it's wrapped as well as possible to keep any extra air out. Store in the refrigerator until leaving for an outdoor adventure. For short-term storage, it can be carried in a pack about one month. For long-term storage, keep refrigerated.

Other forming options include pouring pemmican into a greased cake pan and cutting into cubes or forming it into a dozen 1-inch balls. Store in plastic bags or enclose each in canvas or muslin casing so it resembles old-fashioned plum pudding. Or dip the balls or logs in melted paraffin to seal and make watertight.

Makes 4 cups.

PEMMICAN PARFLECHES

1 cup coarsely chopped jerky
1 cup coarsely chopped dried cranberries
¾ cup coarsely chopped dried wild plums
¾ cup coarsely chopped dried cherries
1½ tablespoons red-wine vinegar
1 tablespoon finely chopped fresh thyme
1 tablespoon finely chopped fresh rosemary
¼ cup thawed, frozen orange juice concentrate
30 sheets (12 by 17 inches each) phyllo dough
2 cups melted butter
Bread crumbs

This recipe was inspired by L'Etoile's Savory Purse of American Bison and Wisconsin Wild Plum. I have adapted it by using orange juice and Herb Jerky, although any jerky will work. Don't miss the opportunity to select this from the L'Etoile menu, if you have the chance.

Note: Drizzle a mixture of ⅔ cup thawed frozen orange juice concentrate and ⅓ cup honey over warm parfleches.

Combine the first 8 ingredients. Set aside and allow time for the ingredients to evenly moisten. Place one phyllo sheet on a clean, dry work surface. Brush a light layer of butter, starting with edges, then painting the entire surface. Sprinkle a fingerful of bread crumbs over the sheet. Crumbs serve as something between each layer to ensure flaky phyllo dough. Use 5 sheets phyllo dough and build 5 layers in this manner. Use scissors to cut this stack into 4 pieces, 6 inches wide and 8 ½ inches long (2 cuts each way). Place 1 rounded tablespoon jerky mixture in the center and fold phyllo edges into the center to form a "purse." Use melted butter to bind dough together. Repeat this process with remaining phyllo sheets. Bake 15 to 20 minutes at 400 degrees until golden. Serve as an entree. Makes 24 pieces.

JERKY BOUILLON

Jerky can be hard to chew for both young and old people. Native Americans ground it into powder, mixed it with hot water and drank it, much like we do coffee as a morning beverage. The Celts of Armorica and the nomads of Asia Minor did the same thing. In 1680, a guy by the name of Martin developed a drink made from powdered jerky and water—called Martin's Broth.

⅓ cup powdered or shaved jerky
1 cup water

Mix together and allow 5 to 10 minutes for flavors to blend. Use boiling water for faster rehydration. Uncooked, rehydrated jerky should be refrigerated if not used within one hour.

Makes 1 cup.

Homemade bouillon or consomme is easy to make. Various meat and fish jerkies offer a spectrum of flavors. Grind jerky into powder in a blender or shave it with a sharp knife. Generally speaking, 3 to 4 jerky strips, each 5 inches long and 1 inch wide, grinds to ⅓ cup.

JERKY DIP

¾ **cup powdered jerky**
¼ **cup yogurt**
1 package (8 ounces) cream cheese
1 teaspoon finely chopped green onions
½ **teaspoon minced garlic**
¼ **teaspoon fresh lemon juice**

In a bowl, stir all ingredients together. Cover and refrigerate for flavors to blend for at least one hour.

Makes 2 cups.

Any jerky, including fish, can be used to make this dip. Use with crackers, potato chips, raw vegetables or dried tomato chips or spoon on top baked potatoes. Low-fat and non-fat versions of yogurt and cream cheese can be used. For variety, add 1 tablespoon roasted garlic and 1 teaspoon dried tomato powder.

JERKY PUFFS

Just about any type of jerky can be used to make this party appetizer. My first choice is Teriyaki Tuna Jerky on page 67.

¼ cup ground jerky, cut in ½-inch pieces
½ cup shredded cheddar cheese
¼ cup mayonnaise
⅛ teaspoon freshly ground black pepper
2 egg whites
24 crackers
Paprika to sprinkle

Mix together jerky, cheese, mayonnaise and pepper. Let sit 15 minutes for flavors to blend. Whip egg whites stiff. Gently fold whites into jerky mixture. Place crackers on a cookie sheet. Spoon 1 teaspoon of mixture on top each cracker. Sprinkle with paprika. Place under the broiler until the tops turn golden brown. Serve hot.

Makes 24.

NILES' JERKY OMELET

2 tablespoons powdered jerky
2 tablespoons water
4 eggs
2 tablespoons salsa
1 tablespoon chopped green onion

Combine jerky powder and water. Let sit 5 minutes. Whip eggs. Add rehydrated jerky. Heat pan and add mixture. When omelet is just about done, add green onions. Top with salsa.

Makes 2 servings.

Niles Deden is my brother-in-law. He's the guy in the family who's known for making great breakfasts. When he sampled some of the jerkies at a family gathering, he was eager to start cracking those eggs and adding various jerkies. This is his best shot. My favorite jerkies to use in this recipe are Bloody Mary Jerky on page 39 and Ham Jerky on page 59. Cholesterol-free Egg Beaters® work as well as fresh chicken eggs.

JERKY HASH

Grandpa's Vension Jerky on page 38 is particularly good to use in hash. *Grandma likes to make this hash as a way to use leftover baked potatoes.*

½ cup jerky, cut in ½-inch pieces
¼ cup water
1 tablespoon olive oil or butter
3 cups peeled and sliced raw potatoes
½ cup chopped celery
2 tablespoons jerky bouillon
3 chopped green onions
½ teaspoon minced garlic
Salt and pepper to taste

Rehydrate jerky in water 10 minutes, drain and save jerky-flavored (bouillon) water. Over high heat, add oil, potatoes, celery and 2 tablespoons of the reserved jerky bouillon. Reduce heat to medium, cover and cook until potatoes are soft. Remove lid and add onions, garlic, salt and pepper. Stir to prevent sticking.

Makes 4 servings.

JERKY CORN CHOWDER

2 medium potatoes, diced in ½-inch cubes
2 cans (14½ ounces each) chicken broth
2 cups Tasajo Jerky, cut in ½-inch pieces
1 cup chopped onion
1 teaspoon minced garlic
1 tablespoon butter
1½ cup chopped celery
¼ cup chopped fresh parsley
1 bay leaf
1 teaspoon paprika
1 package (10 ounces) frozen cut corn, thawed
¼ cup brandy
½ cup thick cream
¼ teaspoon freshly ground black pepper

My friend Lee Weiss is not only a fantastic watercolorist, but she's also the best soup maker in town. When I asked her for a soup recipe, she was intrigued with using Tasajo Jerky on page 51. The cornmeal coating on the Tasajo is enough to thicken the stock. This is a hearty meal in a dish. Serve with a good loaf of bread and you have it all.

Dice potatoes, rinse and let stand in 1 can chicken broth. Soak jerky in 1 can chicken broth at least 30 minutes. In a 4-quart kettle, saute onions and garlic in butter until transparent but not brown. Add celery and saute 1 minute more. Add parsley. Add jerky and stock in which it was soaked, bay leaf and bring to a boil, reduce heat to low and keep just under simmer for one hour. Add potatoes, paprika and stock. Bring to boil. Reduce heat and simmer uncovered until potatoes are cooked. Add corn, brandy and cream. Heat but do not boil. Add pepper. Makes 8 servings.

JERKY CASSEROLE

Just like the old standby, tuna casserole, this recipe can be put together in the morning before work, refrigerated and popped in the oven for dinner. I use Soleful Jerky on page 71 and it's hard to tell it was ever dried fish.

½ cup jerky, broken into small pieces
1 cup milk
1 cup dry macaroni
2 cups water
1 can (10¾ ounces) cream of mushroom soup
¾ cup frozen peas
1 tablespoon finely chopped onion
¼ teaspoon freshly ground black pepper

Place jerky and milk in a 1-quart casserole dish and allow to rehydrate at least 15 minutes. In a separate pan, cook macaroni in water. Drain macaroni. Add soup, peas, onion and pepper and macaroni to rehydrated fish. Stir. Bake at 350 degrees 30 minutes.

Makes 4 servings.

JERKED GOULASH

1 can (28 ounces) tomatoes
½ cup jerky, cut in ½-inch pieces
1 tablespoon olive oil
1 cup chopped (¼-inch dice) onion
1 teaspoon minced garlic
1 teaspoon dried basil
½ teaspoon dried oregano
1 cup uncooked shell or elbow macaroni
Salt and pepper to taste

Put tomatoes in a soup pot. Squeeze tomatoes with your hands into smaller pieces. Add dried meat, stir and let rehydrate at least 30 minutes. Place olive oil, onions and garlic in a frying pan and saute on high heat until thoroughly cooked. Add seasonings. Reduce heat to medium low and cook 5 to 10 minutes to evaporate some of the liquid. Remove from heat. Add to tomatoes. Cook pasta in a separate pan. Drain. Mix ingredients together.

Makes 2 servings.

Although this recipe is especially good using poultry jerky, any ground meat jerky or strips, including vegetarian jerky, can be used. This makes a great backpacking meal. Once you reach your destination, add water, heat and serve.

BACKPACKER GOULASH

While at home, follow the preceding recipe, but leave out jerky and do not add macaroni. Store jerky in one plastic bag and macaroni in another. Once cooked, spread the mixture evenly on lightly oiled roll-up sheets and place in a dehydrator until thoroughly dry. Store in airtight bags. Label with name and date. Weighs 4 ounces dried and measures about 2 cups. Shelf life is one month or keep refrigerated 6 months or frozen indefinitely.

4 cups water
2 cups dried goulash
½ cup jerky, cut in ½-inch pieces
1 cup uncooked shell or elbow macaroni

Tear dried goulash into 1-inch pieces. Soak dried goulash and jerky pieces in 2 cups water at least thirty minutes. Warmed water decreases rehydration time. In a separate pan, bring 2 cups water to a boil over high heat. Add macaroni and cook until done. Once jerked goulash has rehydrated, cook over medium heat until excess liquid evaporates (about 5 minutes). Stir occasionally. Add drained, cooked macaroni, stir, cover and remove from heat. Let sit 10 minutes. Stir and serve.

Makes 2 servings.

JERKY VEGETABLE SOUP

3 cups water
½ cup jerky, cut in ½-inch pieces
2 cups potatoes, cut in ¼-inch chunks
1 cup zucchini, diced in ¼-inch pieces
1 cup tomato, chopped in ¼-inch pieces
½ cup onion, chopped in ¼-inch pieces
¼ cup mushrooms, diced in ¼-inch pieces
¼ cup bell pepper, diced in ¼-inch pieces
1 teaspoon salt
1 teaspoon garlic
¼ teaspoon powdered dried sage
¼ teaspoon freshly ground black pepper
¼ teaspoon cayenne pepper
1 bay leaf

I've been making this soup ever since I started backpacking in the Big Horn Mountains more than 20 years ago. It's been a great meal to look forward to on canoe and fishing trips and has become a family favorite. Although it's made with meat, we consider it a low-fat meal and when vegetarian jerky is used, it's a fat-free dish.

Put water and jerky in a large pot and rehydrate 30 minutes. Hot water speeds the rehydration process. Add all remaining ingredients. Cover and cook over medium heat until all ingredients soften. Remove bay leaf.

Makes 2 servings.

BACKPACKER VEGETABLE SOUP

While at home, make jerky vegetable soup, but leave out jerky and reduce water to 2 cups. Spread evenly on a lightly oiled roll-up sheet and thoroughly dry in a dehydrator. Store dried ingredients in one airtight bag. Label with name, date and weight. Dried weight is 4 ounces and measures 2 cups. Shelf life is one month. Seal and refrigerate up to 6 months.

2 cups dried vegetable soup
½ cup jerky, cut in ½-inch pieces
3 cups water

Put dried vegetable stew, jerky and water in a pan and rehydrate 30 minutes. Warm water speeds rehydration. Slowly bring to a boil over medium heat. Stir. Cover, remove from heat and let sit an additional 15 to 30 minutes to finish rehydrating and cooking. Add more water if necessary.

Makes 2 servings.

PASTA CON CARNE SECA

⅔ cup jerky, cut in ¼-inch pieces
⅓ cup cream
2 tablespoons melted butter
8 ounces uncooked fettuccine, spaghetti or penne
Shredded Parmesan cheese
Coarsely cracked black pepper to taste

Place jerky pieces, cream and melted butter in a bowl. Let stand at room temperature 30 minutes. Prepare pasta according to package directions. Drain and add to jerky mixture. Toss well. Top with Parmesan cheese and black pepper.

Makes 2 servings.

This recipe was developed by Peter and Maureen Beck. The marinade he used to make his jerky is on page 48. It's a rich and flavorful main course that can be served for a very special occasion.

119

JERKY CELERY SLAW

Make this slaw ahead of time when planning on packing the picnic basket with potato salad and beans. Or serve on top fresh garden greens as a jerky-kind-of-salad.

1 can (15 ounces) peas, drained
1 can (15 ounces) French-cut green beans, drained
1½ cups finely chopped celery
1 cup seeded and chopped green pepper
1 cup chopped onion
1 jar (4 ounces) pimiento pieces
¾ cup sugar
⅓ cup canola oil
1 cup cider vinegar
2 tablespoons water
1 teaspoon minced garlic
¼ teaspoon paprika
¼ teaspoon salt
¼ cup jerky, cut in ¼-inch pieces

In large mixing bowl, combine the first 6 salad ingredients. In small mixing bowl, blend together the next 7 dressing ingredients. Pour dressing over salad. Refrigerate overnight. One hour before serving, add jerky.

Makes 12 servings.

WINDY CHILI

1 cup chopped onion
½ cup water
1 teaspoon dried oregano
1 teaspoon dried basil
1 tablespoon minced garlic
1 cup chopped celery
1 cup chopped green pepper
1½ cups crumbled jerky
1 quart (32 ounces) V-8® juice
2 teaspoons chili powder
1 can (15 ounces) black beans
1 can (15 ounces) chickpeas (garbanzo beans)
1 can (15 ounces) kidney beans
1 can (28 ounces) tomatoes
¼ teaspoon Tabasco®
⅛ teaspoon freshly ground black pepper

This started out as spaghetti sauce but the day was windy and cold and it turned into a "spaghetti, no, chili for a windy day" memory. The beginning of a chile recipe is very similar to spaghetti sauce. Simply add the first 8 ingredients, then substitute a 15-ounce can of tomato sauce for V8®, do not add any beans and serve over cooked spaghetti. Spicy Tomato Soy Jerky is a good jerky to use for this recipe.

In saute pan, cook onion in water with oregano, basil and garlic. Add celery and green pepper and reduce heat to simmer until vegetables are cooked, about 5 minutes. Transfer to stock pot and add crumbled jerky, V-8, chili powder, black beans, chickpeas, kidney beans, tomatoes (crush, if necessary), Tabasco and pepper. Simmer, uncovered, at least ½ hour. Serve over cooked potatoes or pasta, if desired. Makes 12 servings.

JERKY AND BLACK BEANS

A guy in Des Moines asked if I had a recipe using jerky with black beans. I asked my friend Lee Weiss, who makes delicious black beans, to help with this recipe. Red wine is needed to beef up the jerky. She served it over cooked rice, with a salad, succotash, a robust bread and flan for dessert. Her rendition was hearty, filling and simple.

1 pound dried black beans
8 cups water
1½ cups jerky, cut in ½-inch chunks
¼ cup olive oil
2½ tablespoons minced garlic
2 cups chopped onion
2 green, large, sweet chili peppers, finely chopped without seeds
1 tablespoon salt
1 teaspoon freshly ground black pepper
¼ teaspoon ground cumin
¼ teaspoon dried oregano
2 tablespoons sugar
2 bay leaves
½ cup dry red wine
1½ tablespoons vinegar
4 cups cooked rice

Sort and discard any imperfect beans. Wash. Cover and soak overnight in water. In the morning, drain, rinse with fresh water and drain again. Soaking tones down gas from beans. Place water in a kettle and add beans. Bring to a rapid boil. Reduce heat to moderate, cover and cook 1 hour. Remove 1 cup cooked beans with a slotted spoon, mash and set aside. Add jerky to cooked beans and hot juices. Cover and let stand.

In a medium-size saucepan, add oil and saute garlic, 1½ cups of the chopped onion and peppers over medium-low heat until soft and mashable, but not browned. Mash with potato masher 1 cup cooked beans. Add to sauteed mixture and mash all ingredients thoroughly.

Add this mixture to the kettle. Add salt, pepper, cumin, oregano, sugar and bay leaves. Cover and boil 1 hour over moderate heat. Reduce heat to low. Add wine and vinegar. Simmer over low heat 1 more hour.

Uncover, remove bay leaves and cook until sauce thickens.

Serve over cooked rice and top with remaining ½ cup chopped raw onions.

Makes 8 servings.

CREAMED JERKY

Chipped beef was once the most popular dried meat in the stores. In the '50s and '60s, we used to buy it to make creamed chipped beef on toast. Just about any type of jerky can be shaved with a knife into thin pieces and substituted for store-bought chipped beef. Serve over toast, muffins, cooked potatoes, rice or pasta. This dish is even better if sauteed mushrooms, green peas and minced onion are added.

1 cup jerky, cut into ¼-inch pieces or shaved
½ cup water
2 tablespoons butter
1 tablespoon flour
1 cup milk
¼ cup shredded cheddar cheese
½ teaspoon freshly ground black pepper

Rehydrate jerky in water at least 15 minutes in a saucepan. Bring to a boil for 5 minutes, taking care that the liquid doesn't completely evaporate. Remove jerky from pan and put in a bowl. Melt butter in pan. Add flour. Brown butter and flour. Stir constantly to prevent scorching. Add milk. Stir. Cook over low heat until thickened. Add jerky and continue stirring. Remove from heat. Add cheese and pepper.

Makes 2 to 4 servings.

BACKPACKER CREAMED JERKY

1 cup jerky, cut into ¼-inch pieces or shaved
1 cup cold water
⅓ cup powdered milk
2 tablespoons butter
1 tablespoon flour
¼ cup fat-free Parmesan cheese
½ teaspoon freshly ground black pepper

Rehydrate jerky in water at least 15 minutes in a saucepan. Bring to a boil for 5 minutes, taking care that the liquid doesn't completely evaporate. Remove jerky from pan and put in a bowl. Melt butter in pan. Add flour. Brown butter and flour. Stir constantly to prevent scorching. Mix water and powdered milk. Add milk. Stir. Cook over low heat until thickened. Add jerky and continue stirring. Remove from heat. Add cheese and pepper.

Makes 2 to 4 servings.

For variety add ¼ cup dried mushroom slices and/or dried green peas to the rehydrating jerky. When you add more dried foods you will need to increase the water and also give it a little more time to rehydrate. Consider adding a tablespoon of dried peppers and dried minced onions.

JERKED RICE

Cook jerky along with rice. Once cooked, use as a base for rice and veggies or simply add small pieces of fresh vegetables for crunch, such as bell pepper.

2¼ cups water
1 cup short-grain brown rice
¼ cup jerky, cut in ¼-inch pieces
2 tablespoons dried tomato pieces, broken in ¼-inch pieces
1 tablespoon olive oil
¼ teaspoon dried basil
¼ teaspoon dried oregano

Combine all ingredients and simmer covered 20 to 30 minutes. A rice cooker is a great appliance to use for making great rice every time.

Makes 4 servings.

JERKY BREAD

1 loaf raw bread dough
½ cup jerky, chopped into ¼-inch pieces
2 tablespoons water
1 teaspoon finely ground black pepper

Mix dough. In a small bowl, mix jerky, water and pepper and let sit at least 15 minutes. Add to dough and bake.

For this recipe, use either a box of commercial bread machine mix or make your own dough.

You can have an entire sandwich in a loaf of bread. Add dried pieces of tomato, onion and a strip of jerky. Or use Ham Jerky, dried tomato slices and wrap in a piece of crisp lettuce. Just think cheese and jerky bread. The creative potential is limitless— and fun. Odessa Piper from L'Etoile liked the idea so much, she developed a jerky croissant for the Saturday Madison Farmers' Market crowd.

SALMON JERKY LOAFETTES

My mother-in-law Adeline Deden has been making salmon loaf since she started cooking with her mother almost 70 years ago. She is a creative and adventurous cook and jumped at the chance to make this recipe with dried salmon. The Honeyed Salmon Jerky recipe on page 65 is perfect for this recipe.

1 cup Honeyed Salmon Jerky, broken into ½-inch pieces
½ cup milk
2 beaten eggs
2 tablespoons melted butter
½ cup cracker crumbs
2 tablespoons chopped fresh parsley
¼ teaspoon salt
¼ teaspoon freshly ground black pepper

Put jerky pieces in milk and let sit at least 30 minutes. Add next six ingredients. Spoon in six greased cupcake forms or bake in a greased loaf pan or casserole dish. Bake 20 minutes at 350 degrees. Cool and serve with sauce.

Makes 6 servings.

SALMON LOAFETTE SAUCE

2 tablespoons butter
4 tablespoons chopped onion
2 tablespoons flour
1 cup half-and-half
1 cup milk
1 cup thawed, frozen peas
1 tablespoon mushroom pieces

This sauce is wonderful and can be served over cooked potatoes.

Melt butter and add onion. Cook until onion is translucent. Add flour. Stir. Add half-and-half and milk. Stir until thickened over medium heat. Add peas and mushrooms. Serve over baked Salmon Jerky Loafettes on page 128.

Makes 6 servings.

JERKY CAKE

When I told my friend and editor Annie that I wanted to include a jerky cake in this book, she said I'd lost my marbles. Well, maybe so, but I'll bet it's a hit at a birthday party. How about a chocolate jerky cake?

A good choice is the Fruity Jerky on page 45. Grind jerky when it's cold. At room temperature, it's sticky and more difficult to grind.

½ cup dried jerky powder
1 box (16.75 ounces) 1-step angel food cake mix

Make angel food cake according to instructions on box. Add jerky powder after the cake is completely blended. Stir only enough to mix thoroughly. Bake according to box directions. Cake should cool before frosting.

Makes 12 servings.

JERKY FROSTING

1 package (7.2 ounces) fluffy white frosting
2 tablespoons ground jerky
1 teaspoon shredded jerky

What's a cake without frosting? My mom's answer to this question is "sweet bread."

Follow frosting box directions. Once frosting is completely mixed, add jerky. Frost cake and dribble shredded jerky over the top (like shredded chocolate or coconut).

Frosts one angel food cake.

JERKY ICE CREAM

Jerky Ice Cream was inspired by L'Etoile's Peppercorn Ice Cream. I tried this with both soft-serve custard and ice cream using Hot Jerky strips and ground meat jerky. The amount of jerky may vary depending on the type selected. What is most interesting about this is that it's both cold and hot at the same time. My friends Lee Weiss and Carol Tarr suggested mixing lemon sorbet with a tart jerky to use as a jerky palate cleanser.

1 pint ice cream
2 tablespoons finely ground jerky
⅛ teaspoon finely ground black peppercorns

Remove ice cream from container. Place in a larger container with a tight-fitting lid. Use a knife to cut ice cream into smaller pieces. Add jerky and pepper and mix. Cover the container and freeze immediately. Serve in small tablespoon dollops with fresh fruit or on frosted jerky cake.

Makes 4 to 8 servings.

INDEX